D0935246

Solid Wastes
Management

Solid Wastes Management

The Regional Approach

Kenneth C. Clayton
John M. Huie

Ballinger Publishing Company ● Cambridge, Mass.
A Subsidiary of J.B. Lippincott Company

Library
I.U.P.
Indiana, Pa.

658.92844   C578 s
C. 1

Copyright © 1973 by Ballinger Publishing Company. All rights reserved. No part of this publication may be reproduced, stored in a retrieval system, or transmitted in any form or by any means, electronic mechanical, photocopy, recording or otherwise, without the prior written consent of the publisher.

Library of Congress Catalog Card Number: 73-9584

International Standard Book Number: 0-88410-300-5

Printed in the United States of America

Library of Congress Cataloging in Publication Data

Clayton, Kenneth C
    Solid wastes management.

Bibliography: p.
1. Refuse and refuse disposal—Indiana. 2. Regional planning—Indiana.
I. Huie, John M., joint author. II. Title.
TD788.C56   658'.92'844   73-9584
ISBN 0-88410-300-5

Contents

List of Figures

List of Tables

Foreword

Accompanying the growing concern with the environment has come a strongly expressed desire of communities to deal with solid wastes in a more satisfying systematic and economical way. Like any other environmental problem, there are multiple goals to be achieved, and there is a variety of ways to meet the goals depending on local conditions. There is no best way to meet waste disposal objectives that is independent of city size, character of residents, industry and topography.

In addition to the many engineering and attitudinal considerations encountered in decisions on how to dispose of wastes, there are complex cost considerations which involve alternative methods of disposal, e. g. as between incineration and landfill, routing, equipment and location of disposal sites. The present study pioneers in applying sophisticated optimization techniques to the problem of solid waste disposal for a city and its surrounding counties. The beginnings of the study are typical in that a community became dissatisfied with the environmental conditions associated with its open burning dump. What is not typical is that in seeking solutions they came in contact with economic researchers from Purdue University who helped explore the possibilities of a regional solution. The researchers were able to apply programming tools for simultaneous optimization of routing and sites.

There has been too much delay in giving serious attention to economic problems connected with solid wastes. Hopefully, this study will lead the way to many more studies in an area long neglected by economists.

George S. Tolley

University of Chicago

Acknowledgments

We wish to give special thanks to Dr. Arlo Minden and Dr. Henry Wadsworth for their helpful review of an earlier draft of this text. Thanks also to Dr. Joseph Havlicek, Jr., for his perceptive critique of an earlier version of Chapter 4. The disposal cost data in Chapter 4, moreover, would have been difficult to synthesize without the assistance of Mr. William Pullen, Manager of Product Improvement, Whayne Supply Company, Louisville, Kentucky.

We also wish to acknowledge Dr. Andrew Whinston and Dr. Robert Noonan for use of the Noonan-Whinston routing algorithm. In addition, it was Dr. William Caudle and his staff at Combinatorics, Inc., Lafayette, Indiana, that provided the programming expertise necessary to make the Noonan-Whinston algorithm operational in the context of this book.

Finally, we would like to recognize Purdue University for the support it has provided throughout the duration of our research.

Chapter One

Introduction

In recent years man has become increasingly aware of his environment and the effect he has upon it. The depletion of natural resources and the pollution of air and water have received considerable attention as examples of the need for concern. An equally important aspect of man's effect on the environment is the solid wastes that he generates and the methods that he uses to dispose of them.

The trend in solid wastes output in the United States has been one of continual increase, both on a per person basis and in terms of absolute quantity (see Figure 1-1). Coupled with this mounting output—and compounding the problem—has been a widespread incidence of disposal facilities with a propensity for environmental degradation.[1] Permitted to continue unchecked, this situation could, indeed, leave man the victim of his own progress.

Fortunately, efforts are being made to improve the standards for solid wastes handling. Much remains to be done, however. The knowledge that is required for rational decision-making has yet to be fully developed.

SOLID WASTES DEFINED

Generally speaking, "waste is a material that its producer does not want. Although the product may have value to someone (either in its present or in a converted state), if its producer does not ask for reimbursement for its removal it is considered to be waste, and at some stage, will enter a waste handling system, either private or public."[2] Solid wastes, within this context, are defined to be the nongaseous and nonliquid wastes that result from the daily activities of a community's residential, commercial, and industrial sectors. As such, they are classified primarily according to garbage, ashes, and rubbish. Garbage is said to

1

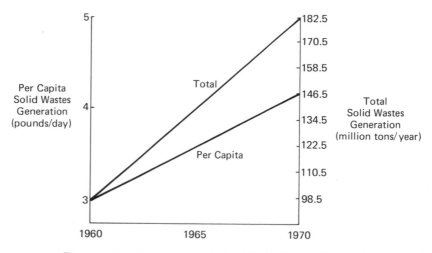

Figure 1-1. Per Capita and Total Solid Wastes Generation, United States, 1960–1970 Source: Adapted from T.R. Miller, *Solid Waste Management*, Division of Planning, Department of Commerce, State of Indiana, 1971.

include the organic matter that results from the preparation and consumption of foods. Ashes are the residue that remains after various cooking and heating processes. Rubbish is a loosely defined category that consists of most solid wastes not included in the other two categories. Rubbish may take the form of combustibles, including paper, rags, wood, leaves and weeds, or noncombustibles, such as glass and metal materials.

THE CASE FOR REGIONAL SOLID WASTES MANAGEMENT

It has been observed that when the solid wastes problem first "reached critical proportions in the 1960's, jurisdictional arrangements, economic concepts, social attitudes, and technology were all found ill-suited"[3] to its resolution. With the recent increase in water management and air pollution control programs, the disposal of solid wastes in a manner consistent with environmental criteria has become more urgent.

The problems connected with the increasing volume of solid wastes

> have been recognized in many cities and metropolitan areas, and efforts are being made to find solutions. However, solid waste problems are by no means confined to cities and large metropolitan areas. Failure to recognize solid waste problems in rural areas may be one

reason why open dumps, open-dump burning, and littering occur
and are making many rural areas lose their advantage over cities in
environmental quality. As urban frontiers penetrate deeper into rural
areas, solid waste problems in rural areas will become more critical. . . . The need for attention to solid wastes is accentuated by the
fact that governments in rural areas are not as well equipped in man-
power, expertise, and other resources to deal with solid waste problems as are governmental units for cities and larger metropolitan
areas.[4]

Economic theory suggests that at least certain of the disadvantages
being faced by rural governments may be overcome if economies of regionalization are realized. In particular, solutions to the solid wastes problem may be
forthcoming if a regional approach is adopted. As noted elsewhere,

the set of options available for solving the solid waste handling problems increases as the size of the geographic areas is enlarged. Among
the factors supporting this statement are (1) greater available economic resources and opportunities to achieve economies of scale,
and (2) the presence of sufficient land resources which can be dedi-
cated to the needs of solid waste disposal.[5]

If such advantages can, in fact, be gained from regional systems of
solid wastes management, it is important that the potential for regionalization be
explored. The empirical evidence advanced thus far has been less than adequate.
Additional information is required if a meaningful evaluation is to be made of
the economic feasibility of regional solid wastes management.

THE PROBLEM

Evansville, Indiana, and a small fringe area surrounding it, presently receives
solid wastes collection service, the collected wastes being disposed of at a sanitary landfill located within the city limits. Many of the smaller towns and most
of the rural areas in the counties of Vanderburgh, Posey, Gibson, Pike, Warrick,
and Spencer in Indiana and Henderson County in Kentucky receive no such
service. As a result, the residents of this Southwestern Indiana and Kentucky
Council of Governments region must either burn or dispose of their solid wastes
in open dumps, publically operated and otherwise, or in illegal roadside dumping
areas. The burning of solid wastes contributes to air pollution, however, and
open dumping is unsightly and unsanitary. The disposal methods with the widest
application in this region fail to meet environmental criteria and are unaccept-
able. The State of Indiana has recognized the objectionable nature of existing

methods and as of January 1, 1971, open dumps and open-dump burning have been forbidden by law.[6]

The problem, then, is to determine what system of solid wastes disposal should be adopted by the Southwestern Indiana and Kentucky Council of Governments region. Potential alternatives are necessarily restricted to those that satisfy environmental criteria.

THE PURPOSE

As previously indicated, it is possible—from a theoretical standpoint—that a regional system of solid wastes disposal may enjoy certain economies of operation not normally available to smaller individual systems. It is the general purpose of this book to test this hypothesis. A regional solid wastes system will be evaluated for the Southwestern Indiana and Kentucky Council of Governments region.

Specific objectives to be realized include:

1. The determination of the optimal individual system of solid wastes disposal for each of the counties in the Southwestern Indiana and Kentucky Council of Governments region.
2. The determination of the optimal regional system of solid wastes disposal for the Southwestern Indiana and Kentucky Council of Governments region.
3. The determination of the optimal system of solid wastes disposal for the Southwestern Indiana and Kentucky Council of Governments region.

THEORETICAL CONSIDERATIONS: LOCATION THEORY

The basic problem in this study is one of locating solid wastes disposal facilities. An optimal pattern of disposal site location is sought for the members of the Southwestern Indiana and Kentucky Council of Governments. In order to decide what is optimal, however, it is first necessary to have a uniform set of location criteria. Alternative sets of criteria are provided by *location theory*.

Location theory has passed through four stages of development.[7] These phases include: (1) the least-cost location phase; (2) the nearness of markets phase; (3) the profit-maximization phase; and (4) the least-cost to customers phase.

Least-Cost Location Phase

Least-cost location theories specify that a firm will locate so as to minimize its costs of production and distribution. The distinguishing characteristic of this type of theory is its formulation within a purely competitive framework. Demand for the firm's product is assumed to be completely elastic, no matter where the firm is located.

One of the original contributions to least-cost location theory was made by Johann vonThunen.[8] VonThunen's theory directs itself to the effect that transportation costs have on the allocation of land resources between alternative agricultural uses. It is assumed that a single consuming center is situated within an isolated state. The land surface is said to be homogeneous and the productivity of labor is assumed to be uniform for the various agricultural outputs.

Land use is shown to occur in concentric zones surrounding the consuming center. Price differentials between zones are attributed to differences in transportation costs. Those land uses which incur the highest transportation costs tend to locate closest to the consuming center and receive the highest prices. Products with less expensive rates of transfer are produced at greater distances from the center and receive lower prices when sold. Profit margins are equalized by land rents which are negatively correlated with distance from the consuming center.

An equally important theory of least-cost location has been advanced by Alfred Weber.[9] This theory differs from vonThunen's in its relaxed assumptions of a heterogeneous land surface and more than one consuming center. Moreover, Weber's model includes three factors which are said to influence the location decision: (1) transportation costs, (2) labor costs, and (3) agglomerating forces.

If the transportation costs are isolated as the only relevant factor, the site with the lowest total transfer cost is chosen. The exact location of this minimum transport-cost site with respect to raw materials deposits and consuming centers is a function of each particular product's characteristics.

Weber goes beyond vonThunen's theory with the recognition that labor cost may often influence a location decision. The effect of this labor factor may be such that it causes an adjustment in the transfer cost-minimizing location. Such an adjustment in location is made when the savings in labor cost outweigh any increase in transportation cost.

The third factor included in Weber's model is agglomerating forces, both positive and negative. Positive forces include the various economies that are associated with size of operation, improved marketing channels, and proximity to tertiary industries. Diseconomies such as higher site rents also fall into this category and are viewed as negative or disagglomerating forces.

An important point to note about Weber's analysis is the absence of institutional and special factors. In developing a theory general enough to apply to all industrial location decisions, he has excluded such factors as insurance, interest, taxes, climate, and management.

A third major least-cost location theory is the work of Edward M. Hoover.[10] Hoover suggests certain demand determinants as well as cost factors but formulates his theory largely within the framework of costs. Cost factors are separated into (1) transportation costs and (2) production costs.

The importance of Hoover's analysis rests on his inclusion of institutional factors and with the degree of detail with which he examines the various costs and their respective impacts. Locational choice is shown to be a problem of substitution among costs of production and transportation; the objective being to minimize the total of these expenses. Specifically, in choosing among alternative locations, the Hoover model adjusts, by accepting a slightly higher production cost if it means a greater reduction in transportation cost and vice versa.

Nearness of Markets Phase

The nearness of markets phase in the development of location theory signals the introduction of more realistic concepts. Assumptions on the distributions of population and raw materials, the type of competition, and the interdependence of firms within a multimarket economy are relaxed. Consumers are pictured as being scattered over an area and not confined to a single consuming center. Production costs are assumed to be identical (as opposed to least-cost theory) with sale price based on the distance between the firm and its customers. By locating throughout an area, sellers are assumed to be able to gain control over the customers nearest to their plants. This type of theory is an outgrowth of monopolistic competition analysis, with sellers locating so as to maximize their respective shares of a given market demand.

When the assumptions of the nearness of market location model are such that the size and shape of a firm's market area are derived on the basis of assumed locations, it is said that a *market-area* approach is being adopted. Typical of this approach is a theory developed by August Losch.[11] The Losch model assumes a broad homogeneous plain that is dotted with completely self-sufficient farmsteads, uniform transportation features in all directions, and an even scatter of raw materials deposits.

Based on these assumptions, Losch finds a hexagon with a plant in the center to be the most nearly perfect market-area shape; the distance to consumers is minimized and the share of market demand is maximized. At equilibrium, given the hexagon market-area, each producer maximizes profits (with marginal revenue equal to marginal cost) and the number of independent selling units is maximized, with all areas being served by at least one firm.

The trading areas of the various products are viewed as nets of hexagons. The size of a net is a function of each particular product's characteristics. When these nets are rotated about a common center, the result is six sectors with large numbers of production centers and six sectors with very few such centers. The coincidence of a great number of these centers tends to concentrate population, minimize transport costs, and provide a larger selection of goods—all factors which, in turn, cause industry to agglomerate to an even greater degree.

If the nearness of market location theory seeks to find the reasons for a particular location decision, a *locational interdependence* approach is being used. This approach assumes freely movable locations so that the attraction or repulsion of a firm in response to the presence of a competitor at a given location may be examined. A classical theory of this type has been contributed by Harold Hotelling.[12]

In order to consider the spatial interdependence of locations, Hotelling assumes an even scattering of consumers, an infinitely inelastic demand for the industry's product, equal assembly, production, and distribution costs at all locations, a perfectly competitive market, and a sale price exclusive of transportation costs. With a linear market area, Hotelling's model indicates that firms will concentrate at the center of the market. With reference to Figure 1-2, it may be noted that each firm (*A* and *B*) has an incentive to move toward the other to expand its respective share of the market. If *A* located to the right of *M*, however, *B* could locate just to the left of *A* and obtain the larger share of the market. Similarly, *A* could gain the larger share of the market if *B* located to the left of *M*. The only possible point of equilibrium, therefore, is at *M* in the center of the market, and this is where both *A* and *B* will locate.

Profit-Maximization Phase

The third phase in the development of location theory is the profit-maximization phase. This phase is concerned with the hypothesis that the firm's optimum location is determined by the difference between total revenue and total cost. The major contributor to this aspect of location theory has been Melvin L. Greenhut.[13] The Greenhut model separates location factors into

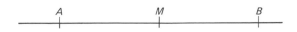

Figure 1-2. Hotelling's Locational Interdependence Model

four major categories: (1) transportation costs, (2) production costs, (3) the demand for a product, and (4) cost reducing and revenue increasing factors.

The general theory developed by Greenhut is actually a synthesis of the earlier least-cost and nearness of markets theories. The result of this combination is a theory which specifies location decisions on the basis of profit maximization. In mathematical form this theory appears as:

$$(1)\ L = (\ T - C\ )$$
$$(2)\ C = (\ S \cdot A\ )$$
$$(3)\ T = (\ S \cdot P\ )$$

where L is the location, C is total cost, T is total revenue, S is sales radius, which by definition is proportional to sales, A is the average cost exclusive of freight, and P is the profit maximizing net mill price.

According to this model, locational equilibrium is said to exist when the average cost is equal to the net mill price (average cost equals marginal revenue) and marginal cost is equal to marginal revenue. If net mill price is greater than or less than average cost, even if marginal cost is equal to marginal revenue, a state of disequilibrium will exist. Since the natural tendency of the system is assumed to be toward a state of equilibrium, it follows that any changes in net mill price or average cost will cause a reactionary movement within the system toward locational equilibrium.

Least-Cost to Customer Phase

The least-cost to customer phase is the most recent in the development of location theory. It is similar to the profit-maximization phase except that decisions are based upon the delivered cost to customers rather than net mill prices. The criterion of delivery time to consumers as it relates to delivered cost finds wide application. Also, considerable emphasis is placed on the use of analytical models such as linear programming.

One such least-cost to customer model is the work of Walter Isard.[14] Following the Weber-Hoover philosophy, Isard derives a single best location primarily on the basis of transportation costs.

Another theory of this type has been advanced by Leon N. Moses.[15] The Moses formulation is very similar to Greenhut's in that each considers both demand and cost factors as they affect site location. However, while Greenhut solves directly for maximum profit, Moses searches for the minimum cost associated with a given level of investment. Through the principle of duality, of course, the end results of Greenhut and Moses are identical.

Disposal Site Location Criteria

The important factors which affect location decisions have been identified as location theory has evolved. Of these, the criteria set forth during the least-cost location phase appear most appropriate for the solid wastes location problem. Only the processing and transportation cost factors need be considered. Institutional factors, among others, need be included only as constraints on the cost-minimization problem, or insofar as they affect the selection of possible alternatives during the formulation of the model.

SOCIAL WELFARE CONSIDERATIONS

As noted above, the costs of transportation and disposal are the theoretical determinants of a solid wastes disposal site location decision. The usual disposal cost function includes such costs as the wages and salaries of personnel, equipment owning and operating expense, and administration and overhead charges. In cases where the disposal site is not operated in a proper and sanitary manner, however, the usual cost function will most likely understate the true cost of disposal. In effect, a joint service is being provided when such conditions prevail—a salable disposal service and a nonsalable "disservice," namely pollution.

When underground water supplies are polluted, open burning is permitted to foul the air, and the infrequent application of cover material allows odors to permeate the countryside, a cost is imposed upon those who are affected by such conditions. For example, the preliminary findings of a study of the impact of disposal site location on property values indicate that oftentimes "solid waste disposal sites are sources of adverse external effects which are borne by owners of surrounding properties."[16] A study city, which had dumps and unsanitary landfills, provided the information "that for a degree away from downwind of a solid waste disposal site the value of a piece of residential property increases $12.10. The estimated coefficient for the distance variable suggests that the price of residential property increases 69 cents per foot of distance away from a solid waste disposal site."[17]

A dichotomy due to externalities thus exists between the private and social costs of solid wastes disposal. The rectification of this situation is no easy matter. "In general, the economic approach seeks to transform the social costs of production and marketing to individual (private) costs, so that the price of every marketable product will reflect its full costs of production to the economy."[18] The primary means for achieving this transformation appear to be taxation or the imposition of effluence charges, subsidies, and the redefinition of waste disposal standards.[19]

It is important that the social costs of solid wastes disposal not be overlooked. For the purposes of this study, however, it is assumed that disposal is performed in compliance with revised standards and that the social costs due to adverse externalities are negligible.

GENERAL PROCEDURES

An analysis of the problem under study—namely, whether a regional system of solid wastes disposal is the least-cost alternative—requires the application of the same selection procedure to several cases. In particular, a least-cost disposal system must be developed for each of the counties and for the Southwestern Indiana and Kentucky Council of Governments region as a whole. Once these least-cost systems have been determined, they can be compared in terms of dollar costs to establish the disposal system that is, in fact, the least-cost alternative.

Before any such comparisons can be made, however, there are several other matters that must be considered. A rural collection system must be designed, as no such system presently exists in the study region. A cost function for collection vehicles must be estimated so that transportation costs can be calculated. Similarly, a long-run cost function for the disposal of solid wastes must be estimated. Finally, potential sanitary landfill sites for local and regional systems must be selected. Only when these requirements have been accomplished, will it be possible to assess the economic feasibility of regional solid wastes management in the Southwestern Indiana and Kentucky Council of Governments region.

NOTES

1. See A.J. Muhich, A.J. Klee, and P.W. Britton, *Preliminary Data Analysis—1968 National Survey of Community Solid Waste Practices*, Public Health Service Publication No. 1867, Washington, U.S. Government Printing Office, 1968.

2. N. Morse and E.W. Roth, *Systems Analysis of Regional Solid Waste Handling*, U.S. Department of Health, Education and Welfare, Public Health Service, Environmental Health Service, Bureau of Solid Waste Management, 1970, p. 1.

3. C.G. Golueke and P.H. McGauhey, "First Annual Report," *Comprehensive Studies of Solid Waste Management—First and Second Annual Reports*, U.S. Department of Health, Education and Welfare, Public Health Service, Environmental Health Service, Bureau of Solid Waste Management, 1970, p. 1.

4. J. Havlicek, G.S. Tolley, and Y. Wang, " 'Solid Wastes'—A Resource?," *American Journal of Agricultural Economics*, Vol. 51: No. 5, p. 1598.

5. Morse and Roth, *op. cit.*, p. 20.

6. J.M. Huie, *Solid Waste Management-Storage, Collection and Disposal*, Cooperative Extension Service, Purdue University, Lafayette, Indiana, 1970, pp. 13-24.

7. R. Reed, *Plant Location, Layout and Maintenance*, The Irwin Series in Operations Management, Richard D. Irwin, Inc., Homewood, Ill., 1967, pp. 3-7.

8. J.H. vonThunen, *Der Isolierte Staat in Beziechung auf Landwirtschaft und Nationalokonomic*, 3rd edition, Schumacker-Zardilin, Berlin, 1875.

9. C.J. Friedrich, *Alfred Weber's Theory of the Location of Industries*, University of Chicago Press, Chicago, 1928.

10. E.M. Hoover, *The Location of Economic Activity*, McGraw-Hill, New York, 1948.

11. A. Losch, *The Economies of Location*, as translated by William H. Woglom and Wolfgang F. Stolper, Yale University Press, New Haven, Connecticut, 1964.

12. H. Hotelling, "Stability in Competition," *The Economic Journal*, Vol. 39: No. 153, pp. 41-57.

13. M. Greenhut, *Plant Location in Theory and in Practice – The Economics of Space*, The University of North Carolina Press, Chapel Hill, North Carolina, 1956.

14. W. Isard, *Location and Space Economy*, John Wiley & Sons, Inc., 1956.

15. L. Moses, "Location and the Theory of Production," *Quarterly Journal of Economics*, Vol. 73, pp. 259-272.

16. J. Havlicek, R. Richardson, and L. Davies, *Measuring the Impacts of Solid Waste Disposal Site Location on Property Values*, Urban Economics Report No. 65, The University of Chicago, 1971.

17. *Ibid.*, p. 12.

18. J. Scherer, "Pollution and Environmental Control," *Federal Reserve Bank of New York – Monthly Review*, Vol. 53: No. 6, p. 134.

19. *Ibid.*, pp. 134-135.

Chapter Two

Methodology

It was indicated in the previous chapter that certain key factors are thought to exert a considerable influence on location decisions. In the case of solid wastes management, the location choice is primarily influenced by the combined costs of collection and disposal. Institutional factors such as environmental regulations and political interests are recognized as having an effect but mainly as constraints on—rather than as determinants of—the decision problem. Further, location decisions within the context of solid wastes management are said to be made on the basis of cost-minimization. The mathematical and empirical decision models developed for this study, consequently, follow a least-cost approach.

The purpose of this chapter is to outline the model that will be used to evaluate the economic feasibility of a regional system of solid wastes disposal. As a basis for this presentation the physical processes or activities that comprise a solid wastes system are reviewed first. This descriptive analysis is then reformulated in terms of quantitative relationships to form a general or theoretical framework. Finally, the empirical model to be used in the analysis of the regional solid wastes system is presented as an extension of the theoretical framework.

SOLID WASTES MANAGEMENT SYSTEM

The satisfactory disposal of solid wastes requires a highly integrated and professionally operated system. Such a system will include three processes or activities: (1) storage, (2) collection, and (3) disposal.

Storage

Storage is the first activity in a solid wastes management system. Solid wastes must initially be amassed at the site where they are generated in order for collection and disposal to be successfully accomplished. In areas where population is highly concentrated the distances between sites will be short enough to permit on-site storage. When the distances between sites are increased, however, it often becomes more economical to consolidate solid wastes at one or more common collection points. In rural areas such collection points most often take the form of strategically located collection bins.

Collection

The second activity in a solid wastes system is collection. The collection process includes the removal and transport of solid wastes to a disposal site. This activity is often quite expensive as it can involve several pieces of equipment and a large number of personnel. It is apparent, moreover, that the productivity of each collection vehicle and its crew will be dependent upon the amount of time spent in transit. The distance between each origin of solid wastes and each disposal site, as reflected in the collection cost, is thus a primary determinant of the disposal site location decision.

Disposal

Disposal, the third activity in a solid wastes system, provides for the destruction and/or final removal of solid wastes. Present technology is such that several disposal alternatives are feasible from an engineering standpoint. The relevant methods, however, are those which satisfy the standards that have been established by the Indiana State Board of Health.

The most frequently used of these relevant methods are the sanitary landfill and incineration. "The sanitary landfill is presently the only true disposal method and is basic to any solid wastes program. Incineration is a volume reduction process and produces residues which should be sanitary landfilled."[1] Grinding, composting, pyrolysis, high temperature incineration, and salvaging and recycling techniques are used less often but may find increased application as the state of the art is advanced.

The sanitary landfill is generally considered to be the most economical of the relevant disposal alternatives. As a disposal process, the sanitary landfill provides for the spreading and compaction of solid wastes in shallow layers of not more than two feet in depth. Each of these layers is covered with six to eight inches of soil at the end of the day's operations, or more frequently if required. A completed landfill receives a final two foot cover of soil.

This sanitary landfill process can be performed in either of three variations. The *area* method is best used when natural depressions exist at the site. The major limitation of this variation is that cover material must be hauled in or obtained from an adjacent area. Use of the *trench* method eliminates the cover material problem. Solid wastes are placed in a trench which has been dug for that purpose and are covered with the soil that was originally excavated. A final variation is the *ramp* method. In this case, a natural slope or grade at the site is utilized. Solid wastes are dumped on this slope and spread, compacted, and covered with soil. In order to avoid making unwarranted assumptions about the geographical and geological characteristics of the study area, the more generally applicable trench method of sanitary landfilling is assumed.

The second principle determinant in a disposal site location decision, then, is the cost of disposal at a sanitary landfill.

In summary, a solid wastes system consists of three physical processes or activities: storage, collection, and disposal. The determinants of a disposal site location decision are the collection cost and the cost of disposal at a sanitary landfill.

THE GENERAL MODEL

Once the determinants of a least-cost location decision have been identified, it becomes a matter of incorporating them into a general model or theoretical mathematical framework. Such a framework provides a concise and consistent statement that may be subjected to analytical evaluation.

The cost of the collection activity includes the expenses associated with both the collection and transportation of solid wastes. It is represented as follows: [2]

$$\sum_i C_{ij}^c = \sum_i C_{ij}^T (X_{ij})$$

where: C_{ij}^T = the per ton-mile transport cost for solid wastes transported between the ith origin and the jth disposal site.

X_{ij} = tons of solid wastes transported from the ith origin to the jth disposal site.

Disposal costs, the second determinant of a solid wastes disposal site location decision, are of the form:

$$C_j^D = f_j (W_j)$$

where: W_j = the total volume of solid wastes disposed of at the jth disposal site.

The disposal site location decision is made so as to minimize the combined costs of collection and disposal. This total system cost at the jth disposal site is:

$$TC_j = C_j^D + \sum_i C_{ij}^c$$

and the total system cost for all J disposal sites (in case $j > 1$) is:

$$TC = \sum_j TC_j = \sum_j C_j^D + \sum_i \sum_j C_{ij}^c$$

There are certain logical restrictions which must also be introduced into this cost-minimization framework. These constraints include:

(1) The jth disposal site cannot dispose of more solid wastes than its maximum physical capacity will permit or

$$T_j = W_j + T_j^*$$

(Maximum disposal capacity = solid wastes disposed of + unused disposal capacity.)

(2) All j disposal sites cannot receive more solid wastes from origin i than are generated at origin i or

$$\sum_j X_{ij} = G_i$$

(Total volume of solid wastes received by all j disposal sites from origin i = total volume of solid wastes generated at origin i).

(3) The jth disposal site must dispose of the same volume of solid wastes that it receives or

$$W_j = \sum_i X_{ij}$$

(Total volume of solid wastes disposed of at disposal site j = total volume of solid wastes received at disposal site j from all origins i).

The method of Lagrange's Undetermined Multipliers can be used to minimize the total cost of transportation and disposal subject to the restrictions specified above. In Lagrangian form the function to be minimized appears as:

$$TC^* = \sum_j f_j(W_j) + \sum_i \sum_j C_{ij}^T(X_{ij}) - \sum_j \lambda_j(T_j - W_j - T_j^*)$$

$$- \sum_i B_i(\sum_j X_{ij} - G_i) - \sum_i \gamma_i(\sum_j W_j - \sum_j \sum_i X_{ij})$$

where TC^* is a new total cost function which can be minimized subject to the constraints. The values which minimize TC^* will also minimize TC.[3]

The first-order conditions for the minimization of TC^* are seen to be:

$$\frac{\partial TC^*}{\partial W_j} = f'_j(W_j) + \lambda_j - \gamma_i = 0$$

$$\frac{\partial TC^*}{\partial X_{ij}} = C_{ij}^{T'}(X_{ij}) - B_i + \gamma_i = 0$$

$$\frac{\partial TC^*}{\partial \lambda_j} = (T_j - W_j - T_j^*) = 0$$

$$\frac{\partial TC^*}{\partial B_i} = (\sum_j X_{ij} - G_i) = 0$$

$$\frac{\partial TC^*}{\partial \gamma_i} = (\sum_j W_j - \sum_i \sum_j X_{ij}) = 0$$

Rearranging these results yields:

$$f'_j(W_j) + C_{ij}^T(X_{ij}) + \lambda_j - B_i = 0$$

or

$$f'_1(W_1) + C_{i1}^T(X_{i1}) + \lambda_1 - B_i = 0$$

$$f'_2(W_2) + C_{i2}^T(X_{i2}) + \lambda_2 - B_i = 0$$

$$f'_J(W_J) + C_{iJ}(X_{iJ}) + \lambda_J - B_i = 0$$

In order for the total cost of a solid wastes system to be a minimum, therefore, the necessary conditions are that the combined marginal cost of collection and disposal must be equal among all disposal sites.

The second-order sufficient conditions for a minimum require that at the point defined by the first-order conditions, the second total differential of TC^* be positive:

$$d^2 \, TC^* > 0$$

This requirement assures that the minimum cost for a given volume has been determined. Any adjustments in the input mix can only lead to higher costs.[4]

In summary, the general model that provides a theoretical framework within which the cost of a regional solid wastes system can be minimized is of the form:

$$TC = \sum_j f_j (W_j) + \sum_i \sum_j C_{ij}^T (X_{ij})$$

THE EMPIRICAL MODEL

The general model of the previous section was developed and minimized on the basis of the calculus. The calculus can be applied to those problems in which the quantity to be minimized is stated as a continuous function with continuous first- and second-order partial derivatives. Many real-world problems are not of this form, however. Algorithms are thus developed to facilitate the solution of more realistically formulated problems.

Stollsteimer has developed a procedure for "simultaneously determining the number, size and location of plants that minimize the combined transportation and processing costs involved in assembling and processing any given quantity of raw material produced in varying amounts at scattered production points."[5] The application of the Stollsteimer approach to solid wastes location decisions requires that solid wastes are collected at several origins and then are transported to any of several sites for disposal.

The objective of the Stollsteimer procedure is to determine the least-cost number, size, and location of solid wastes disposal sites. To accomplish this, the objective function, the combined cost of solid wastes transport and disposal, is minimized. Economies of scale are assumed to exist and disposal costs are assumed not to vary among disposal site locations.

Mathematically, the function to be minimized is:

$$TC_{(J, L_K)} = \sum_{j=1}^{J} P_j X_j \,|\, L_K + \sum_{i=1}^{I} \sum_{j=1}^{J} X_{ij} C_{ij} \,|\, L_K \tag{1}$$

(Total cost = Disposal cost + Transport cost)

with respect to disposal site numbers ($J \leqslant L$) and locational pattern $L_K =$ 1 ... ($^{L}_J$). This minimization is established subject to:

$$\sum_{j=1}^{J} X_{ij} = X_i \tag{2}$$

(Sum of collections transported from i to j = Quantity of solid wastes collected at origin i)

$$\sum_{i=1}^{I} X_{ij} = X_j \tag{3}$$

(Sum of collections transported to disposal site j = Quantity of solid wastes disposed of at disposal site j)

$$\sum_{i=1}^{I} \sum_{j=1}^{J} X_{ij} = X \tag{4}$$

(Total collections transported = Total quantity of solid wastes, collected and disposed of)

where: TC = total transport and disposal cost
P_j = unit disposal cost at a disposal site j ($j = 1 \ldots JL$)
X_i = quantity of solid wastes transported from origin i to disposal site j located at L_j
C_{ij} = unit cost of transporting solid wastes from origin i to disposal site j located with respect to L_j
L_K = one locational pattern for J disposal sites among the ($^{L}_J$) possible combinations of locations for J disposal sites given L possible locations
L_J = a specific location for a disposal site ($j = 1 \ldots J$).

There are two steps involved in minimizing the objective function with respect to disposal site numbers (J) and location pattern (L_K). The first step is to obtain a transport-cost function that has been minimized with respect to disposal site locations with varying numbers of disposal sites, J. Mathematically, this function is as follows:

$$TTC_J = L_K^{min} \, (X_i) \, C_{ij_{L_K}} \qquad (5)$$

where: TTC = total transport cost minimized with respect to disposal site locations for each value of $J = 1 \ldots L$

(X_i) = a (1×1) vector where entries, X_i, represent the quantities of solid wastes produced at each of the I origins

$C_{ij_{L_K}}$ = a vector where entries C_{ij} represent minimized unit transport costs between each origin and a specified set of locations, L_K, for J disposal sites.

The second step in this procedure is to add the disposal cost to the minimized transport-cost function for each value of J (the number of disposal sites). The number of disposal sites that minimize the combined transport and disposal costs will depend on the relative slopes of the two functions.

The accomplishment of the first step—to obtain a transport-cost function that has been minimized with respect to disposal site locations and numbers—is achieved in this study with the aid of a computer assisted vehicle scheduling routine that has been developed by Noonan and Whinston. "Although the system was designed specifically for scheduling trucks, it is applicable wherever a routing based principally on time constraints must be determined."[6] As a traffic schedule, "the basic task of the system is to create the routes that the vehicles should follow in order to satisfy customer demands. The resulting assignment minimizes the number of vehicles used and the total distance traveled by each vehicle. Thus, the total distance traveled by the fleet is effectively minimized."[7]

The solution to this vehicle routing system is obtained through the use of a classification algorithm. The algorithm proceeds by selecting a collection point on the perimeter of the collection points to be serviced. A collection vehicle, originating at the disposal site, is routed to this initial collection point and is then directed to the next closest collection point. This process of routing by measure of closest association is continued within specified time and load limit constraints. If a full load should be realized prior to the time constraint, the collection vehicle is returned to the disposal site for emptying and then sent back out to continue servicing collection points until the time constraint is reached. The result of this procedure is an optimal route design for a specified set of collection points.

When the least-cost transportation patterns associated with varying numbers of disposal sites have been established, the volume of solid wastes to be handled at each disposal site can be determined. The disposal costs that are associated with these volumes and, thus, with the transportation patterns can be calculated. Potential solid wastes systems can then be compared on the basis of their respective combined transport and disposal costs to establish the identity of the least-cost system.[8]

NOTES

1. National Association of Counties Research Foundation, *Solid Waste Management-Design and Operation (No. 5)*, U.S. Department of Health, Education and Welfare, Public Health Service, Consumer Protection and Environmental Health Service, Environmental Control Administration, Bureau of Solid Waste Management, 1969, p. 10.

2. It is assumed that summations over i, j and k range from 1 to I, 1 to J, and 1 to K respectively.

3. For a detailed review of this method see, for example, J.P. Lewis, *An Introduction to Mathematics*, St. Martin's Press, New York, 1965.

4. For a more detailed consideration of 1st- and 2nd-order conditions see P.A. Samuelson, *Foundations of Economic Analysis*, Atheneum, New York, 1967, pp. 57-89 and Appendix A; J.M. Henderson and R.E. Quandt, *Microeconomic Theory—A Mathematical Approach*, McGraw-Hill Book Company, New York, 1958, pp. 49–54 and Appendix A.3.

5. J.F. Stollsteimer, "A Working Model for Plant Numbers and Locations," *Journal of Farm Economics*, Vol. 45: No. 3, pp. 631-645.

6. R. Noonan and A. Whinston, "An Information System for Vehicle Scheduling," *Software Age*, December 1969, p. 8.

7. *Ibid.*, p. 9.

8. There is no theoretical assurance that this "least-cost system" is a global minimum. It is, however, as good a solution as can be obtained. For a discussion of this problem see T.L. Roe, *Optimal Spatial Distribution and Size of Cattle Slaughtering Plants in Indiana*, Unpublished Ph.D. Thesis, Purdue University, Lafayette, Indiana, 1969, pp. 62-73.

Chapter Three

Development of the Solid Waste Systems

The purpose of this chapter is to develop the collection and disposal aspects of the individual county and regional solid wastes systems. Of primary importance is the development of a rural collection system. Basic to this collection system is the determination of the origins and quantities of solid wastes. As a final step, potential disposal site locations are selected and the resulting collection transport distances measured.

THE STUDY AREA

In a practical sense, ". . . whatever the criteria used—geographic, demographic, hydrologic, economic, or community of interest—regions will include several contiguous political entities and will inevitably present an intergovernmental problem if functional unification is attempted."[1] The "fragmentation of authority and responsibility"[2] can often be reduced, however, if an intergovernmental mechanism such as a Council of Governments (COG) is adopted. The region under study is bound together by such a quasigovernmental organization: the Southwestern Indiana and Kentucky Regional Council of Governments. Members of this particular council of governments include the counties of Gibson, Pike, Posey, Spencer, Vanderburgh, and Warrick in Indiana and Henderson County in Kentucky. Only the counties in Indiana are included in this study, however, so as to avoid data collection difficulties and interstate political and legal problems. A map of the study region is presented in Figure 3-1.

The Southwestern Indiana and Kentucky COG region lies in the southwestern section of the state of Indiana. The city of Evansville is the metropolitan hub of the area and, as such, serves as its marketing and trading center. Major highways, including U.S. 41 in a north-south direction and U.S. 460 in an

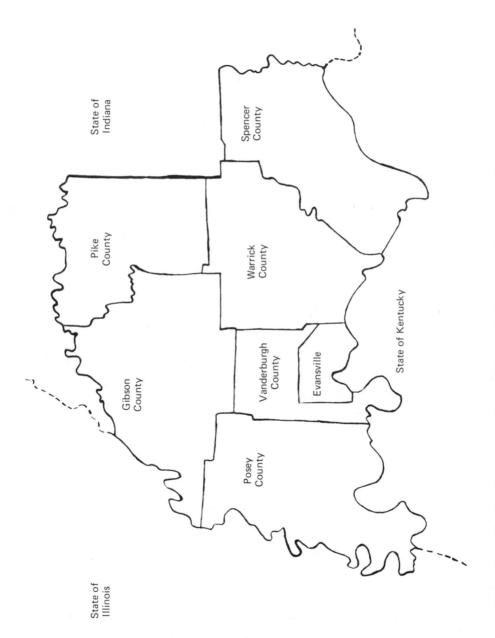

State of
Indiana

Spencer
County

State of
Illinois

Pike
County

Warrick
County

Gibson
County

Vanderburgh
County

Evansville

State of Kentucky

Posey
County

Figure 3-1.   The Southwestern Indiana and Kentucky Council of Governments Region, Indiana, 1971

Library
I.U.P.
Indiana, Pa.

658.92844 C578s
C. 1

east-west direction, provide access throughout the region via Evansville. Interstate 64, presently under construction, will traverse the region in an east-west direction connecting Louisville, Kentucky, and St. Louis, Missouri.

The southern edge of the region borders on the Ohio River. As a result, shipping facilities, primarily at Evansville, provide ready access to water transportation. Air transportation is also available at Evansville and at several smaller airports throughout the region.

According to the 1970 census, the Southwestern Indiana and Kentucky COG area (as used in this study) has a population of 278,343. On a rural-urban basis (urban being greater than 2500 population), there are 104,844 rural residents and 173,499 persons living in urban areas. The city of Evansville constitutes 79 percent of the urban population, however, so that only 24 percent of the remaining population in the region can be classified as urban. Experience suggests the need for some type of rural collection system if state and local regulations against roadside dumps and open-dump burning are to be enforced. A summary of the population and housing numbers in the respective counties of the study region is given in Table 3-1.

In terms of size, the study region includes an area of approximately 3000 square miles. The primary land use in this region is agricultural, and consequently farming provides a considerable, but declining, employment base.

Nonfarm employment is concentrated at Evansville, a diversified manufacturing center. The more important products of this city include such durables as refrigerators, automobile parts, and excavating equipment. The heaviest centers of population in the region are found in and around this major labor market.

Table 3-1. Population and Housing Distributions, Southwestern Indiana and Kentucky Council of Governments Region, Indiana, 1970

| County | Rural | | Urban | |
	Population (number)	Households (number)	Population (number)	Households (number)
Gibson	17,189	5,934	13,255	5,057
Pike	9,584	3,676	2,697	1,162
Posey	14,970	5,059	6,770	2,406
Spencer	14,569	4,581	2,565	910
Vanderburgh	26,296	8,078	143,476	49,933
Warrick	22,236	7,062	5,736	2,078
Total	104,844	34,380	173,499	61,546

Source: Calculated from 1970 Census Medlist Data, U.S. Department of Commerce, Bureau of the Census.

Some of the larger towns and smaller cities, such as Princeton, Petersburg, Oakland City, Mount Vernon, and Boonsville, also offer employment opportunities. As a result, they too have concentrations of population within and around their borders. The remainder of the population is dispersed throughout the region, many of these persons living and working on farms.

SPATIAL DISTRIBUTION OF SOLID WASTES

It is advantageous when considering collection and disposal site location problems to have the spatial distribution of solid wastes generation expressed in terms of some standard unit of area. After careful review of the alternatives, census enumeration districts, as defined by the Bureau of the Census, U.S. Department of Commerce, have been selected. The advantages of such an approach include: [3]

1. The boundaries of census enumeration districts are relatively stable.
2. Secondary source data is easily available for census enumeration districts.
3. Census enumeration districts are sufficiently small to adequately model the real-world situation.
4. Census enumeration districts are contained entirely within major political subdivisions and thus, by appropriate aggregation, the waste generation of an entire political subdivision can be derived.
5. Greater socioeconomic homogeneity is found within a single census enumeration district than exists within the larger political subdivisions.

Estimated Solid Wastes to be Collected

The Census Bureau codes enumeration districts according to a rural-urban classification, the division being made at a population of 2500. Such a distinction lends itself well to a solid wastes study. In particular, the quantities of solid wastes collected are found to differ between urban and rural sources. The average number of pounds of solid wastes collected per person per day in the United States during 1967 was 5.72 in urban areas and 3.93 in rural areas. Of these totals, households accounted for 1.26 pounds in urban areas and 0.72 pound in rural areas. [4]

It is assumed for this study that the collection of solid wastes will increase by fifty percent over a five year planning period. For planning purposes, then, the rural collection of solid wastes is estimated to be at a rate of one pound per capita per day and the urban collection of household wastes is estimated at two pounds per capita per day. Total solid wastes, including business and industrial sources, are estimated to be 8.5 pounds per capita per day in urban areas and 6.0 pounds per person per day in rural areas.

The expected quantity of solid wastes to be collected in each enumeration district can now be determined. In order to calculate this quantity, the population of an enumeration district is multiplied by the appropriate solid wastes collection coefficient (according to the urban-rural classification) to obtain the number of pounds that are collected each day. This quantity is then converted to tons of solid wastes per day, a more usable planning quantity.

Since the amount of solid wastes which must be collected from households is of central importance when designing a rural collection system, the above calculation can also be performed for residential solid wastes alone. A summary of the estimated residential and total solid wastes quantities is provided by county in Table 3-2.

THE RURAL COLLECTION SYSTEM

The development of a rural collection system is based primarily upon the premise that the rural householder carries his solid wastes some distance before disposing of them at an existing unauthorized dump. If such is the case, it seems reasonable to assume that if a suitable container is made available at a distance no greater than that to which the householder is accustomed, he might be expected to deposit his solid wastes in it.[5] Moreover, the stricter enforcement of existing litter laws is possible when an alternative to indiscriminate dumping is provided. In compliance with state regulations, then, solid wastes can be collected periodically and disposed of in an adequate and proper manner.

The Collection Area

The metropolitan area of Evansville, as defined by the Bureau of the Census, is not included in those areas which receive rural collection service, since public and private house to house collection is already being provided. Also,

Table 3-2. Daily Residential and Total Solid Wastes Quantities by County, Southwestern Indiana and Kentucky Council of Governments Region, Indiana, 1971

County	Residential Solid Wastes (tons/day)	Total Solid Wastes (tons/day)
Gibson	21.87	108.00
Pike	7.49	40.23
Posey	14.24	73.61
Spencer	9.87	54.74
Vanderburgh	5.34	32.02
Warrick	16.85	91.06
City of Evansville	150.29	652.40

collection bins are not required for the smaller cities and towns that are incorporated, as they have the taxing power and other legal authority necessary to provide for their own collection service. (It would be feasible, however, to provide
collection service to these incorporated areas if they should require it.) For the
purposes of this study, then, it is the unincorporated towns and rural areas,
which are the responsibility of the respective county governments, for which
provision must be made for the storage and collection of solid wastes.[6]

Storage Bin Requirements

In order to determine the bin requirements of the collection area, it
is necessary to make certain assumptions about the solid wastes that are collected. Specifically, it is assumed that solid wastes are discharged from the collection vehicle at an average density of 400 pounds per cubic yard. This collection vehicle is assumed to have a compaction ratio of 3:1, so that the original
density of the collected wastes must be approximately 134 pounds per cubic
yard. At this density, each four cubic yard bin is capable of holding 536 pounds
of noncompacted solid wastes. These assumptions are supported by preliminary
findings for Chilton County, Alabama.[7]

It must be assumed, at least initially, that only fifty percent of bin
capacity is utilized. This assumption is necessary to allow for periods of peak
waste generation, periods when the average volume may be exceeded considerably. Also, a margin of error must be included to insure against undercapacity.
The usable capacity of each bin is thus assumed to be 268 pounds or 68 pounds
per cubic yard.

It has been noted previously that the rural collection of residential
solid wastes is assumed to be at the rate of one pound per capita per day. Given
the usable capacity of a collection bin, the daily disposal requirements of 268
persons can thus be satisfied with one bin. If it is further assumed that collection
is provided twice per week, it follows that the disposal needs of approximately
75 persons are met by each of the collection bins.

Accordingly, the number of bins required in the rural collection
system is calculated by dividing the population of each of the relevant enumeration districts by 75 (the number of persons served by each bin).

Collection Points

It is possible that, given a concentration of population, more than
one storage bin may be required within a limited area. To simplify the logistics
of collection, several bins may be located at one site. Since the area is small,
residents should not be greatly inconvenienced by any short increases in the

distances to the bins. Bin sites such as these are the collection points of the rural collection system.[8]

The criteria established for the initial selection of collection points for Project Clean and Green, Chilton County, Alabama, include the following:

> Containers should be located near existing unauthorized dumps to take advantage of the householders' operational habits, but they should be far enough away from the dumps to spacially separate the disposal concepts represented by the new containers and the old dumps. They should be located adjacent to the right-of-way of county roads and in places where they would not cause hazardous conditions for people depositing wastes or for the driving public . . . A third criterion was to place a container within ten minutes of driving time of the vast majority of rural homes in Chilton County.[9]

The selection of collection points in this study is best accomplished with the aid of a census enumeration districts map.[10] Such a map is available for each of the counties in the study region. The advantage of this map is the detail which it provides; individual homes, churches, schools, roads, waterways, railroads, and other such features are indicated.

On the basis of the census enumeration districts map, collection points are selected at major intersections, near concentrations of population, and in the weighted centers (weighted by the population distribution) of less populated areas. These points are chosen so that no home is more than four or five miles from a storage bin. The locations of these collection points for each of the study counties are indicated in Figures 3-2 through 3-7.

URBAN COLLECTION

The city of Evansville and the smaller incorporated cities and towns of the study region do not require rural collection service. While the mechanics of the collection systems in these areas are not considered, the quantities of solid wastes collected do have a considerable impact upon the location of disposal sites and must be included in the analysis. In general, the quantities of solid wastes collected from urban households are aggregated for all enumeration districts in a particular city or town, to give the total volumes for each of the cities and towns.

The only exception to this approach is the city of Evansville. In this case, the enumeration districts are divided into unit areas of one square mile

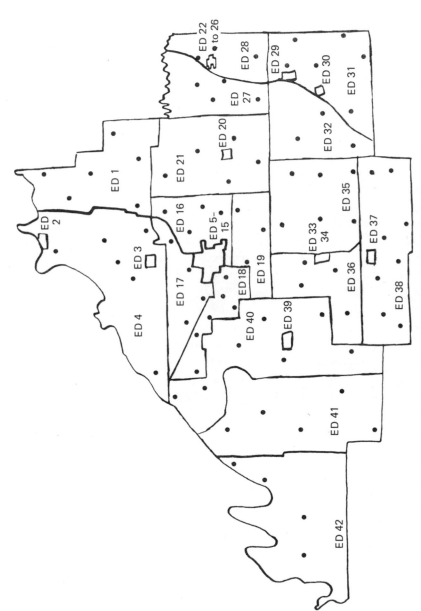

Figure 3-2. Spatial Distribution of Rural Collection Points, Gibson County, Indiana, 1971

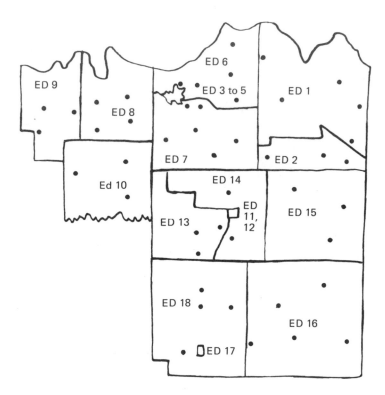

Figure 3–3.   Spatial Distribution of Rural Collection Points, Pike County, Indiana, 1971

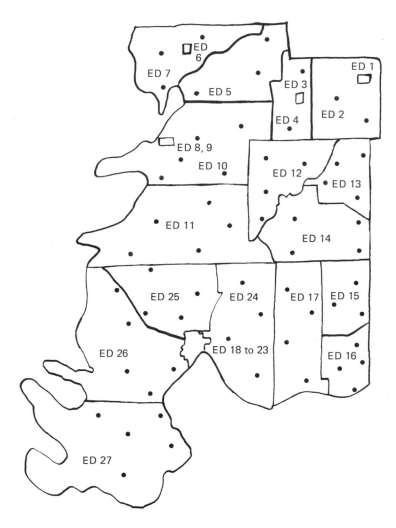

Figure 3–4. Spatial Distribution of Rural Collection Points, Posey
County, Indiana, 1971

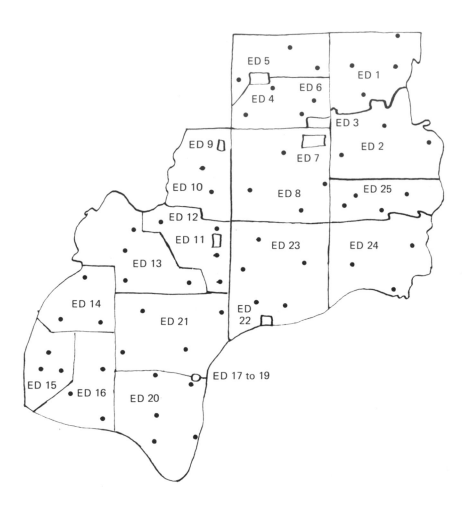

Figure 3–5. Spatial Distribution of Rural Collection Points, Spencer County, Indiana, 1971

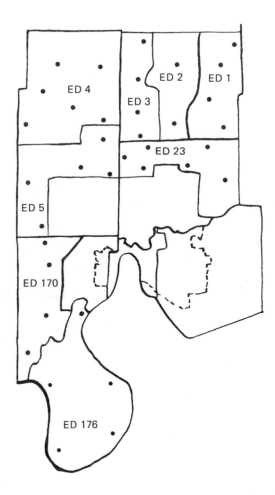

Figure 3-6. Spatial Distribution of Rural Collection Points, Vanderburgh County, Indiana, 1971

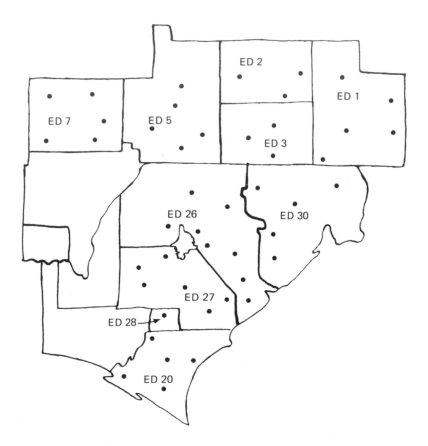

Figure 3–7.   Spatial Distribution of Rural Collection Points, Warrick County, Indiana, 1971

with a collection point at each corner of the area. Solid wastes are assumed to be collected in equal amounts at each of these collection points.

SANITARY LANDFILL SITE LOCATIONS

Location theory suggests that disposal sites should be located so as to minimize the cost of transporting solid wastes. There are, however, certain constraints on the location decision which must be taken into account. Specifically, there are soil and geological considerations which influence the selection of potential sanitary landfill sites.

Geological Considerations

"Solid waste becomes a part of the geological environment . . . when it is deposited in the earth materials of a sanitary landfill, and it is then subject to such normal geologic processes as weathering and movement of water through waste."[11]

Since the degree of detail required for such considerations is not possible in this study, it must suffice to review the most important of the geologic requirements. These requirements have been summarized as follows:

> (1) The base of a proposed landfill should be in relatively fine grained material and more than 20 to 30 feet above the shallowest aquifer.
> (2) The base of a proposed landfill should be above the highest seasonal level of the water table.
> (3) A proposed site should not be subjected to flooding.
> (4) Adequate medium-textured cover material must be available near a proposed site.[12]

It should be noted that these requirements apply primarily to the area method of sanitary landfilling. Requirements (1) and (4) must be compromised in terms of soil-texture in order for the trench or ramp variations of the sanitary landfill to be used.

Soil Considerations

Desirable soil properties for solid wastes disposal by sanitary landfill include those which "(1) prevent leachate from polluting the ground or surface water, (2) hold and absorb any undesirable gases generated by decomposition of wastes, (3) prevent insect or rodent infestation, (4) provide needed aeration and moisture to properly decompose organic wastes, (5) lack stones or rock which would hinder operations, and (6) have the qualities which would not hinder movement of hauling vehicles . . ."[13]

Given these desirable properties, the Soil Conservation Service has developed a series of "limitation classes" which indicate the difficulty of using a particular soil for a sanitary landfill. These limitation classes are generally defined as follows: [14]

Slight: relatively free of limitations or limitations are easy to overcome.
Moderate: limitations need to be recognized, but can be overcome with good management and careful design.
Severe: limitations are severe enough to make use questionable.

The soils in the study region are categorized according to "soil associations." These associations include several soil types and provide a generalized representation of the soils in a particular area. Using soils data provided by the National Conservation Needs Inventory (a 2 percent sampling of quarter-sections in each county as to land use and soils data), it has been possible to characterize the composition of the soil associations and assign limitation classes according to the predominant properties of the soils found to be present. These associations and their limitation classifications are presented in Table 3-3.

Table 3-3. Soil Associations and Limitation Classifications, Southwestern Indiana and Kentucky Council of Governments Region, Indiana, 1971

	Limitation Class		
Association Name	*Slight (percent)*	*Moderate (percent)*	*Severe (percent)*
Wakeland-Stendal-Haymond	5	5	90
Haymond-Nolin-Petrolia	5	5	90
Huntington-Linside	–	10	90
Haymond-Wakeland	5	5	90
McGary	–	20	80
Patton-Henshaw	10	15	75
Patton-Lyles-Henshaw	5	10	85
Peoga-Bartle-Hosmer	10	40	50
Vincennes-Zipp-Ross	5	10	85
Weinbach-Sciotoville	–	–	100
Weinbach-Wheeling	–	–	100
Reesville-Ragsdale	10	50	40
Zanesville-Wellston	25	20	50
Alford	50	30	20
Bloomfield-Princeton-Ayrshire	20	35	45
Hosmer	70	20	10

Source: Calculated from soils data provided by the National Conservation Needs Inventory, Soil Conservation Service, U.S. Department of Agriculture. Calculations made by Dr. Joseph Yahner, Department of Agronomy, Purdue University, Lafayette, Indiana, 1971.

It seems more realistic, for the purposes of this study, to reject certain areas as potential sanitary landfill sites, than it does to accept areas with the understanding that there is only a forty or fifty percent chance of finding a satisfactory sanitary landfill site. Therefore, those soil associations with a 75 percent or greater chance of severe soil problems are excluded from consideration. With these severe soil associations noted on a soil associations map, it is possible to limit potential sanitary landfill sites to those areas most likely to have adequate soil conditions.

Site Locations

It was noted above that sanitary landfill sites should be selected so as to minimize the cost of transportation. These selections, moreover, are restricted to areas other than those which have a 75 percent chance of soil properties that would severely limit the satisfactory operation of a sanitary landfill.

Given the volumes and distribution of solid wastes collected, the cost of disposal at a sanitary landfill, and the cost of solid wastes collection, it is hypothesized that a single-disposal site system will be optimum in the case of each county (and the city of Evansville). Thus, three single-disposal site locations and two dual-site location configurations are considered to test this hypothesis (in the case of Warrick County four single-site locations are considered).[15] The locations of these potential sanitary landfill sites are indicated in Figures 3-8 through 3-13, according to the location code contained in Table 3-4.

The evaluation of a regional system of solid wastes disposal requires that a least-cost system be developed for the study region as a whole, as well as for each of the individual study counties. It is, therefore, hypothesized that the least-cost regional system of solid wastes disposal will have either a single or a dual-site location configuration. In order to test this hypothesis, five single-site, three dual-site, and two triple-site configurations are considered. The sanitary landfill site locations included in these regional configurations are indicated in Figure 3-14, according to the code contained in Table 3-5.

COLLECTION TRANSPORT DISTANCES

The distance measurements between collection points and sanitary landfill sites are made according to the data requirements of the Noonan-Whinston collection vehicle scheduling system.[16] This routing routine requires that each collection point be "linked" with the several nearest collection points and that the distances represented by these links be recorded.[17] Similarly, link measurements are also made between sanitary landfill sites and surrounding collection points.

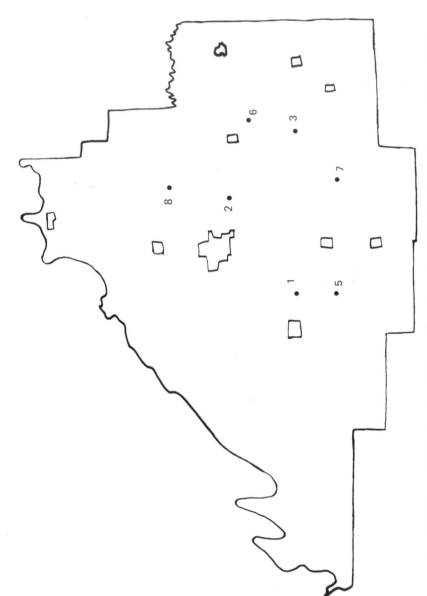

Figure 3-8. Spatial Distribution of Potential Sanitary Landfill Sites, Gibson County, Indiana, 1971

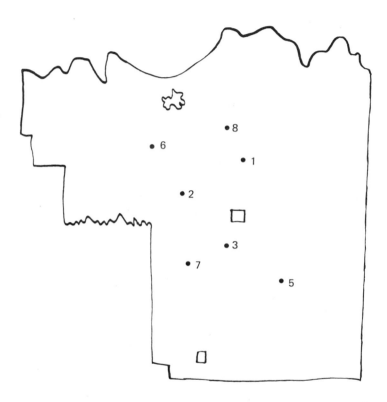

Figure 3–9. Spatial Distribution of Potential Sanitary Landfill Sites, Pike County, Indiana, 1971

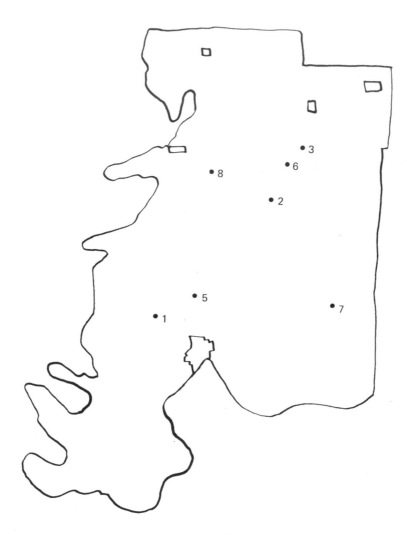

Figure 3-10. Spatial Distribution of Potential Sanitary Landfill Sites, Posey County, Indiana, 1971

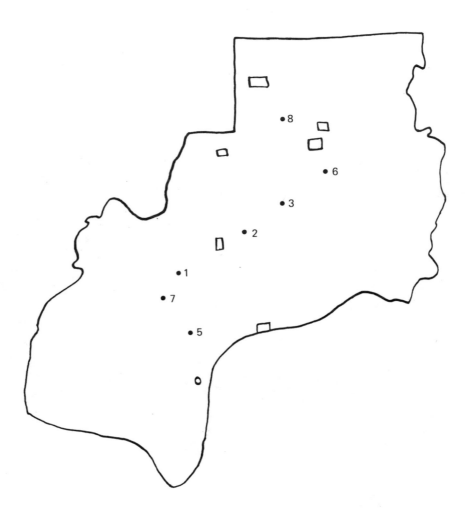

Figure 3-11. Spatial Distribution of Potential Sanitary Landfill Sites, Spencer County, Indiana, 1971

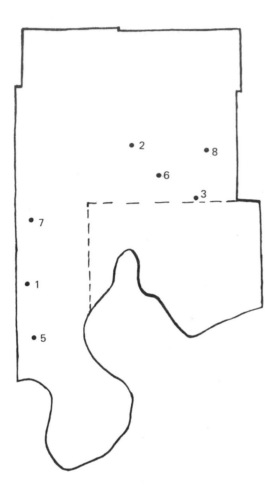

Figure 3-12. Spatial Distribution of Potential Sanitary Landfill Sites, Vanderburgh County, Indiana, 1971

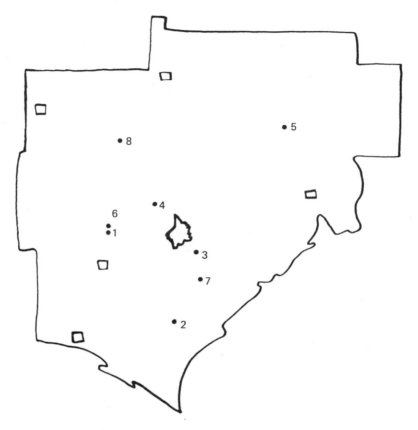

Figure 3-13. Spatial Distribution of Potential Sanitary Landfill Sites, Warrick County, Indiana, 1971

Table 3-4. Potential County Sanitary Landfill Sites Location Code, Indiana, 1971

Site *Configuration*	*Site Code* *Number*
Single-Sites	
Site 1	1
Site 2	2
Site 3	3
(Site 4)*	(4)
Dual-Sites	
Site 1	5
Site 2	6
Site 1	7
Site 2	8

*There is a Site 4 only in the case of Warrick County.

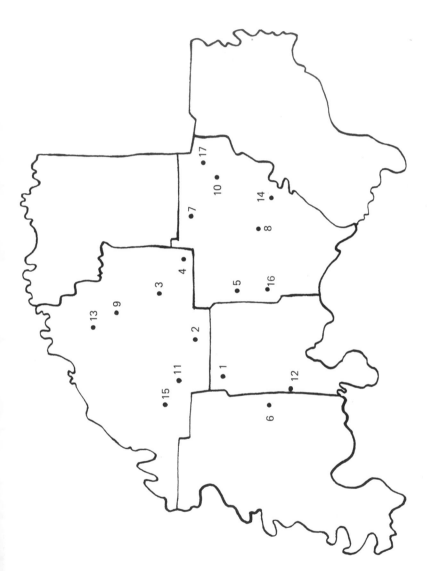

Figure 3-14. Spatial Distribution of Potential Sanitary Landfill Sites, Southwestern Indiana and Kentucky Council of Governments Region, Indiana, 1971

Table 3–5. Potential Regional Sanitary Landfill Sites Location Code, Southwestern Indiana and Kentucky Council of Governments Region, Indiana, 1971

Site Configuration	Site Code Number
Single-Sites	
Site 1	1
Site 2	2
Site 3	3
Site 4	4
Site 5	5
Dual-Sites	
Site 1	6
Site 2	7
Site 1	8
Site 2	9
Site 1	10
Site 2	11
Triple-Sites	
Site 1	12
Site 2	13
Site 3	14
Site 1	15
Site 2	16
Site 3	17

In total, there are 1443 such link measurements needed to formulate the grid system over the study region that is required for the determination of collection vehicle routing.

NOTES

1. R.O. Toftner and R.M. Clark, *Intergovernmental Approaches to Solid Waste Management*, U.S. Environmental Protection Agency, Solid Waste Management Office, 1971, p. 1.

2. *Ibid.*

3. Adapted from N. Morse and E.W. Roth, *Systems Analysis of Regional Solid Waste Handling*, U.S. Department of Health, Education and Welfare, Public Health Service, Environmental Health Service, Bureau of Solid Waste Management, 1970, p. B-8.

4. A.J. Muhich, "Sample Representativeness and Community Data," *An Interim Report 1968 National Survey of Community Solid Waste Practices*, Department of Health, Education and Welfare, p. 13.

5. R.M. Alexander and J.V. Walters, *Chilton County Landfill Summary Report for Initiation Year*, Project Clean and Green, Clanton, Alabama, 1969, pp. 4-5.

6. Note that the collection of solid wastes is performed by each individual county. This will be true in the event of either a county- or a regionally-located sanitary landfill.

7. R.M. Alexander, G.D. Smith, and J.V. Walters, *Chilton County Solid Waste Disposal Demonstration Project Detailed Progress Report*, Project Clean and Green, Clanton, Alabama, 1971, pp. 42-45.

8. In a real-world situation the number of bins placed at a collection point will vary according to traveling habits and the population distribution. For the purposes of this study, however, it is assumed that the quantity of solid wastes collected is the same at all collection points within an enumeration district.

9. Alexander and Walters, *op. cit.*

10. U.S. Department of Commerce, Bureau of the Census, 1970, on the basis of the County General Highway and Transportation Map which has been prepared by the Indiana State Highway Commission, Division of Planning, in cooperation with the U.S. Department of Commerce, Bureau of Public Roads, 1963.

11. N.K. Bleuer, *Geologic Considerations in Planning Solid-Waste Disposal Sites in Indiana*, Environmental Study 1, Geological Survey Special Report 5, Department of Natural Resources, State of Indiana, Bloomington, Indiana, 1970, p. 1.

12. *Ibid.*, p. 7.

13. Preliminary draft of a Soil Conservation Service publication on sanitary landfills, 1971, p. 8.

14. Definitions provided by Dr. Joseph Yahner, Department of Agronomy, Purdue University, 1971.

15. These sanitary landfill sites have been arbitrarily selected given the constraints as reviewed above. The site selections are nonrepetitious in that they do not represent a "pool" of sites from which all possible combinations are evaluated. Actual on-site inspection of the chosen sites was not possible, although the single-site configurations for Warrick County have been approved for use by the Indiana State Board of Health.

16. R. Noonan and A. Whinston, "An Information System for Vehicle Scheduling," *Software Age*, December 1969, pp. 8-13.

17. Teknatronic Applications, Inc., *Data Collection for Computer-Assisted School Bus Scheduling*, Lafayette, Indiana, 1970.

Chapter Four

Synthesis of Cost Data

Location decisions are often made on the basis of transportation and processing costs. This is especially true in the case of solid wastes management. In fact, regional systems of solid wastes disposal find their economic justification when increases in transportation costs are more than offset by decreases in disposal costs.

The purpose of this chapter is to develop the estimated collection and disposal cost functions necessary for the analysis of alternative solid wastes systems. The various cost components which underlie these functions are reviewed and their respective impacts are considered.

A cost function is not established for the storage activity. The cost of this activity does not enter into the location decision, since the same storage system is required for either a county or a regional solid wastes system.

GENERAL CONSIDERATIONS

In practice, every solid wastes system is unique in certain respects, each has characteristics particular to it alone. The various costs for each system reflect this fact and, as a result, no two systems have exactly the same cost structure. Such differences in costs can be attributed, in the case of disposal at a sanitary landfill, for example, to soil characteristics, cover material availability, site topography, types of solid wastes received, and other factors. When developing an actual solid wastes system, then, it must be tailored to fit the existing conditions; a detailed engineering study with specific operational guidelines and cost estimates must be developed for each individual case.

In the present study, such detail is not considered. The development of cost functions for general planning purposes requires that differences between systems be balanced against each other to provide representative cost estimates. It must be emphasized that considerable variability from the estimates given in this study can be expected in a specific case.

The cost estimates for the collection and disposal activities are purposely upward-biased whenever subjective estimation is involved. An upper boundary on costs is more useful and meaningful for planning purposes than is a lower boundary.

The cost data presented in this chapter is reflective of average 1970 prices. Those costs which are synthesized are expressed directly in terms of 1970 dollars. Sample cost data is adjusted in terms of the 1970 price level through the use of the Wholesale Price Index, as computed by the Bureau of Labor Statistics, U.S. Department of Labor.

COLLECTION COSTS

Rural Collection

The storage bins in the rural collection system are assumed to be emptied twice weekly by a thirty cubic yard packer truck which has been specially designed to perform this function. The only crew required to operate this piece of equipment is the driver. Estimated owning and operating expenses are presented below on the basis of information supplied by Project Clean and Green.[1]

The cost of a new thirty cubic yard packer truck of the type used in rural collection is $21,220. Assuming a scrap value of $2,122 and an estimated useful life of five years, the annual depreciation of the truck on a straight-line basis is $3,819.60. The interest, insurance, and taxes on this investment are assumed to total twelve percent of the balance each year, for an average expense of $1,629.70 per year.

The collection system as proposed in this study is county-wide in scope. In each case, the county sanitarian or county engineer is responsible for the satisfactory operation of his county's system. A part of this supervisor's salary must thus be charged against the collection system. It is assumed that twenty percent of an annual salary of $12,000, or $2,400 per year, is a representative amount for this expense.

The driver of the collection truck is generally paid on an hourly basis and, as such, is a variable cost to the system. Adjusted to be representative of the study region, the driver's wage rate is assumed to be $4 per hour.

Other variable costs associated with a rural collection system are provided by previous estimates and include gas and oil at $1.169 per hour, equipment maintenance and repairs at $1.629 per hour, and miscellaneous costs which amount to $0.108 per hour of equipment operation.[2]

A summary of the fixed and variable costs of a rural collection system is presented in Table 4-1. The total annual system cost (assuming twice-weekly or 104 collections per year) is given by a rural collection cost function as follows:

$$C_R^C = \$7849.30 + \$718.224\,(H)$$

where: C_R^C = the total annual cost for a given rural collection system

H = the number of hours required to complete the collection along the system's routes per collection.

Urban Collection

Since the study region includes urban as well as rural areas, it is necessary that the collection costs be adjusted to reflect the equipment and personnel differences of the urban system. One of these differences is the use of a sixteen or twenty cubic yard packer truck instead of the larger thirty cubic yard type used in rural collection. Interviews with local equipment dealers indicate that the cost of a sixteen cubic yard packer truck for use in urban areas is approximately $16,500. Assuming a scrap value of $2,750, the annual depreciation on such an urban collection vehicle, given a five year anticipated useful life, is $2,750. The average annual interest, insurance, and tax charge on this investment is $1,320, when computed at a rate of twelve percent.

Table 4-1. Estimated Annual Rural Collection System Costs, Indiana, 1970

Fixed Costs		
Supervisor's Salary	$2400.00	
Equipment Depreciation	3819.60	
Interest, Insurance, Taxes	1629.70	
Total Fixed Costs		$7849.30
Variable Costs		
Labor	$4.000/hour	
Oil and Gas	1.169/hour	
Equipment Repairs	1.629/hour	
Miscellaneous Costs	0.108/hour	
Total Variable Costs		$6.906/hour

A second major difference in the urban collection system is the inclusion of at least one extra crew member. The services of this laborer are required for the manual emptying of trash receptacles into the packer truck. The wage rate for this position is estimated to be $3.80 per hour, including fringe benefits.

All other fixed and variable expenses are assumed to be identical to those of the rural system. A summary of the urban collection costs is presented in Table 4-2. The total annual cost for the urban collection system is provided by the following urban collection cost function:

$$C_U^C = \$6470.00 + \$10.706 \, (H)$$

where: C_U^C = the total annual cost for a given urban collection system

H = the number of hours required per year for off-route transport to and from a disposal site.

DISPOSAL COSTS

It is assumed here that a sanitary landfill is the most relevant alternative for solid wastes disposal. A cost function is thus estimated only for this particular method of disposal.

As a basis for estimating the disposal cost function it is assumed that the appropriate planning period is five years. Such a period appears to be realistic for planning purposes, as new technology in alternative disposal methods can

Table 4-2. **Estimated Annual Urban Collection System Costs, Indiana, 1970**

Fixed Costs		
Supervisor's Salary	$2400.00	
Equipment Depreciation	2750.00	
Interest, Insurance, Taxes	1320.00	
Total Fixed Costs		$6470.00
Variable Costs		
Labor (Driver)	$4.000/hour	
Labor (Laborer)	3.800/hour	
Oil and Gas	1.169/hour	
Equipment Repairs	1.629/hour	
Miscellaneous Costs	0.108/hour	
Total Variable Costs		$10.706/hour

be expected in the foreseeable future. Also, changes are likely in institutional requirements which will make other alternatives more relevant.

The costs of a sanitary landfill are of two types. Specifically, there is an initial investment which must be made and there is also the yearly cost of operation. The yearly cost of operation includes the interest on the initial investment. An outline of sanitary landfill costs serves to guide the discussion in this section and is presented as follows:

1. Planning and Designing Costs
2. Initial Site Development Costs
3. Land Expense
4. Equipment Owning and Operating Expense
5. Personnel Wages and Salaries
6. Annual Site Maintenance and Development Costs
7. Administration and Overhead Expense

The initial site development and personnel requirements of a county sanitary landfill differ from those of a regional disposal operation. Such differences are, of course, reflected in the respective costs of these two levels of organization. As a result, separate long-run total cost functions must be derived for county and regional sanitary landfills.

Planning and Designing

The careful planning and designing of a solid wastes disposal system is essential if the system is to function successfully when it is placed into operation. Costs must be incurred for legal services, consulting assistance, solid wastes surveys, potential site investigations, and the determination of site engineering specifications. The total of these expenses is assumed to be $50 per ton of initial daily capacity.

With interest at the rate of eight percent on this investment, the average annual planning and designing cost over the five year life of the disposal site can be calculated for each of the various levels of operation. This average annual cost is taken to be representative of the annual planning and designing expense and is presented in functional form as:

$$C_{PD}^{D} = \$12.40\,(V)$$

where: C_{PD}^{D} = the total annual planning and designing cost of a sanitary landfill

V = the daily volume of solid wastes in tons.

Initial Site Development

The costs associated with initial site development differ somewhat between county and regional sanitary landfills. Moreover, these costs are of two varieties at both levels of organization. There are those costs which vary according to the size of the operation and those which are independent of size. The estimates that follow are based on actual costs as reported for Project Clean and Green[3] and on estimated costs contained in the interim report on the *Collection and Disposal of Solid Wastes for the Des Moines Metropolitan Area*.[4]

Site preparation charges vary according to the size of the operation but are unaffected by the level of organization. Typical preparation requirements include the removal of trees, necessary initial grading, and the diversion of any ground water flows. An average cost of $185 per acre is assumed.

Access roadways within the sanitary landfill are essential for a successful operation. Gravel surfacing is often necessary to provide all-weather access to the dumping site. Failure to provide and maintain these roadways in a satisfactory manner can lead to the unnecessary delay of collection vehicles, and could be the cause of an unsanitary accumulation of wastes away from the dumping site during periods of inclement weather. The cost for the installation of these roadways is identical for both county and regional disposal operations and is assumed to be $70 per acre.

Fencing is a very basic item for the successful operation of most sanitary landfills, whether they be county or regional in scope. When erected about the perimeter of a disposal site, fencing serves three purposes. First, it tends to limit access so that the indiscriminant unloading of refuse by passersbys is discouraged. Second, the nuisance of blowing papers is reduced significantly. Finally, accidents resulting from illegal after-hours scavenging are minimized. The expense for fencing is estimated to be approximately $40 per acre.

The public's impression of a sanitary landfill is often vital to its acceptance and successful operation. Frequently mowed grass and a liberal planting of trees and shrubs contribute significantly to the aesthetic value of a disposal site. A *landscaping* cost of $50 per acre is assumed at all levels of organization.

Fixed initial expenses are independent of the size of the disposal operation. One such cost is for an *access roadway into the sanitary landfill*. It is important that this road be constructed so as to withstand the expected traffic volume. Several factors including the materials used, the climate, and the length of the roadway will affect this expense. A representative cost for both county and regional operations is taken as $10,000.

A supply of *water* is required at the sanitary landfill to meet both human and machine consumption needs, as well as for fire protection when municipal fire service is not readily available. The source of this water is either a well at the site or a connection with nearby municipal water lines. In either event, the cost for the provision of water is assumed to be $5,000 at both county and regional operations.

An equipment shed and personnel facility is necessary at all levels of organization, to provide locker space and other facilities for personnel and to protect machinery from undue weather wear. When there is no scalehouse, such a structure will also house the foreman's office. The sophistication of this facility, as reflected in its design and in the materials used in its construction, will vary somewhat according to the size of the disposal operation. At daily volumes of less than 500 tons, a representative cost of $5,000 is assumed. When the level of operation is 500 tons or more but less than 1000 tons per day, a cost of $10,000 is assumed. The cost for this facility when 1000 tons or more of solid wastes are disposed of each day is estimated to be $15,000.

The initial site development costs considered thus far have been equally applicable to county and regional sanitary landfills. In addition to these common requirements, a *scale* and a *scalehouse* are necessary when the disposal operation is regional in scope. These additional facilities are required to provide the means for allocating expenses among participants. The cost of an adequate scale is estimated to be $10,000 and the expense of a scalehouse, which can vary, is assumed to be $10,000.

The estimated initial site development costs for county and regional sanitary landfills are summarized in Tables 4-3 and 4-4, respectively. The totals of these costs at the county and the regional levels of organization, plus interest at the rate of eight percent on the investment, are presented in functional form as indicated in Table 4-5.

Land

The land requirements for a sanitary landfill can be met by use of land already owned, by the purchase of land, or through a land lease. It is assumed in this study that land will be leased for the five year planning period.

The determination of land acreage requirements is basic to the calculation of land leasing expense. The assumptions necessary for the determination of land area needs are: (1) the trench method of sanitary landfilling is used, (2) the depth of the trench is ten feet, and (3) the average of the densities of compaction of solid wastes for all sanitary landfill equipment is approximately 1000 pounds per cubic yard.

On the basis of these assumptions, the first year's land requirements for actual filling are determined. Then, assuming fifty percent increase in the generation of solid wastes over the five year planning period, a 12½ percent

Table 4-3. Estimated Initial Site Development Costs for a County Sanitary Landfill, Indiana, 1970

Fixed Costs		
Access Roadway into the Sanitary Landfill	$10,000	
Water Supply	5,000	
Equipment Shed and Personnel Facility	5,000	
Miscellaneous	10,000	
Total (less than 500 tons per day)		$30,000
Access Roadway into the Sanitary Landfill	$10,000	
Water Supply	5,000	
Equipment Shed and Personnel Facility	10,000	
Miscellaneous	10,000	
Total (500 to less than 1000 tons per day)		$35,000
Access Roadway into the Sanitary Landfill	$10,000	
Water Supply	5,000	
Equipment Shed and Personnel Facility	15,000	
Miscellaneous	10,000	
Total (1000 or more tons per day)		$40,000
Variable Costs		
Site Preparation	$185/acre	
Access Roadways within the Sanitary Landfill	70/acre	
Fencing	40/acre	
Landscaping	50/acre	
Total		$345/acre

increase each year over the first year's land needs must be calculated. Finally, to complete the land requirements estimate, twenty percent of the five year needs or ten acres, whichever is greater, is added to the number of actual fill acres required for five years of operation. These additional acres include the space between trenches, the buffer areas, land used for access roadways into and within the sanitary landfill, and the area needed for a machinery shed, an office, a scalehouse, and other such facilities. The total five year land requirements for the sanitary landfill method of disposal are given by the following expressions, according to the anticipated initial volume:

$$L_1 = 10 + 0.2828 \, (V) \quad 0{-}199 \text{ tons/day}$$
$$L_2 = 0.3393 \, (V) \quad 200{-}1700 \text{ tons/day}$$

where: L = the total number of acres required to operate a sanitary landfill using the trench method for five years

V = the daily volume of solid wastes in tons.

Table 4–4. Estimated Initial Site Development Costs for a Regional Sanitary Landfill, Indiana, 1970

Fixed Costs		
Access Roadway into the Sanitary Landfill	$10,000	
Water Supply	5,000	
Equipment Shed and Personnel Facility	5,000	
Scale	10,000	
Scalehouse	10,000	
Miscellaneous	10,000	
Total (less than 500 tons per day)		$50,000
Access Roadway into the Sanitary Landfill	$10,000	
Water Supply	5,000	
Equipment Shed and Personnel Facility	10,000	
Scale	10,000	
Scalehouse	10,000	
Miscellaneous	10,000	
Total (500 to less than 1000 tons per day)		$55,000
Access Roadway into the Sanitary Landfill	$10,000	
Water Supply	5,000	
Equipment Shed and Personnel Facility	15,000	
Scale	10,000	
Scalehouse	10,000	
Miscellaneous	10,000	
Total (1000 or more tons per day)		$60,000
Variable Costs		
Site Preparation	$185/acre	
Access Roadways within the Sanitary Landfill	70/acre	
Fencing	40/acre	
Landscaping	50/acre	
Total		$345/acre

Table 4–5. Total Annual Site Development Cost Functions, Indiana, 1970

Organization Level	Daily Volume of Solid Wastes		
	0–499 tons	*500–999 tons*	*1000–1700 tons*
County	$ 7440 + 85.56(A)[1]	$ 8680 + 85.56(A)	$ 9920 + 85.56(A)
Regional	$12400 + 85.56(A)	$13640 + 85.56(A)	$14880 + 85.56(A)

1. (A) = the number of acres of land required for a given volume of solid wastes disposal.

Given the physical land requirements, it remains to calculate the associated costs. As the primary land use in the study region is agricultural, it is felt that the value of agricultural land is representative of the cost which must be paid to obtain land for a sanitary landfill. An investigation of land costs in the study area reveals that the average present value of the better agricultural land is approximately $500 per acre. Assuming an annual return of four percent for agricultural use, the average annual return from agricultural land is $20 per acre.

In order for sanitary landfilling to draw land away from agriculture, an annual return in excess of $20 per acre will be required. It is therefore assumed that the necessary land can be obtained for a five year period at $25 per acre per year. The costs associated with various levels of operation are computed according to:

$$C_{L_1}^D = \$250 + 7.0695\,(V) \quad 0{-}199 \text{ tons/day}$$

$$C_{L_2}^D = \$8.4835\,(V) \qquad\qquad 200{-}1700 \text{ tons/day}$$

where: C_L^D = the total annual cost for land at a sanitary landfill

V = the daily volume of solid wastes in tons.

Equipment

The expense associated with the equipment used at a sanitary landfill has a considerable impact upon the total cost of the solid wastes system. The appropriate piece or pieces of equipment for each given size of sanitary landfill must be determined on the basis of estimated machine capacity, as per manufacturer's specifications, and also according to estimated owning and operating costs. A summary of the machine class requirements if provided in Table 4-6. Representative equipment included in each of the machine classes is presented in Table 4-7.

In order to calculate the cost of a given piece of sanitary landfill equipment, it is first necessary to make an "hourly owning and operating cost estimate." Such an estimate can be developed with the aid of handbooks available from equipment manufacturers. Typical costs to be considered are those included in Table 4-8. In making the estimate of fixed and variable equipment costs, it has been assumed that depreciation is straight-line on the basis of hours of operation. An average depreciation period is 10,000 hours. Interest, insurance, and taxes are set at twelve percent of the delivered price.

The expense of the machinery operator is also included as one of the several input costs. An hourly wage rate of $5.00, including fringe benefits, is assumed for all machine classes except 8 and 10 (see Table 4-7). For these latter two classes, $5.30 per hour is assumed. It is further assumed that an equipment operator must be paid for a minimum of eight hours per day, a fixed cost to the

Table 4-6.   Equipment Requirements and Purchase Price of
Equipment by Size of Sanitary Landfill, Indiana, 1970

Volume (tons/day)	Machine Class	Purchase Price[1,2]
0–49	4	$ 35,438
50–149	5	44,006
150–249	6	56,625
250–499	9	77,000
500–1199	9 & 10	122,100
1200–1224	6 & 9	133,625
1225–1624	7 & 9	158,293
1625–1700	8 & 9	191,966

1. Purchase price information provided by Whayne Supply Company (Caterpillar equipment dealer), Louisville, Kentucky.

2. Purchase price for machine Class 10 (dragline) assumes a used piece of equipment.

Table 4-7.   Sanitary Landfill Machinery Classes, Indiana, 1970

Class	Caterpillar	International Harvester	Allis-Chalmers
1	951	150	6G
2	955	175	7G
3	977	250	12G
4	D5	TD-9	HD-6
5	D6	TD-15	HD-11
6	D7	TD-20	HD-16
7	D8	TD-25C	HD-21
8	D9		
9	825 (compactor)		
10	---------------------------	Dragline	------------------

Sources: *Caterpillar Purchasing Guide*, Caterpillar Tractor Company, 1971, *Sanitary Landfill Methods and Benefits*, Allis-Chalmers, Construction Machinery Division, Springfield, Illinois and discussions with equipment dealer representatives.

system for 260 days per year. Overtime compensation for more than eight hours of work per day is at a rate of one and one-half times the regular wage, and is viewed as a variable expense which will be incurred for no more than 250 operating days each year.

Total equipment cost at a given level of operation is computed using the hourly owning and operating cost estimate and the number of hours required for a particular machine to handle a given volume of solid wastes. This time requirement is determined on the basis of the production coefficients contained in Table 4-9. The procedure for calculating the time requirement is to estimate

Table 4-8.   Sanitary Landfill Equipment Hourly Owning and Operating Cost Estimate, Indiana, 1970

1. Delivered Price	_____
2. Less: Resale or Salvage Value	_____
3. Net Depreciation Value (Item 1–Item 2)	_____
Fixed Cost	
4. Hourly Depreciation:	
$\dfrac{\text{Net Depreciation Value (Item 3)}}{\text{Depreciation Period in Hours}}$	_____
5. Hourly Interest, Insurance, Taxes:	
$\dfrac{\text{Annual Interest, Insurance, Taxes}}{\text{Estimated Annual Use in Hours}}$	_____
6. Total Hourly Fixed Cost (Item 4 + Item 5)	_____
Variable Cost	
7. Hourly Fuel: Unit Price × Hourly Consumption	_____
8. Hourly Lubricants, Filters, Grease:	
$\dfrac{\text{Annual Lubricants, Filters, Grease Cost}}{\text{Estimated Annual Use in Hours}}$	_____
9. Hourly Repairs:	
$\dfrac{\text{Annual Repair Cost}}{\text{Estimated Annual Use in Hours}}$	_____
10. Total Hourly Variable Cost (Item 7 + Item 8 + Item 9)	_____
11. *Operator's Hourly Wage*	_____
12. *Total Hourly Fixed and Variable Costs* (Item 6 + Item 10 + Item 11)	_____

the time needed to perform each of the three operations—excavation, spreading, and compacting—involved in the trench method of sanitary landfilling. These time estimates are calculated as follows:

Excavation:

$$\text{Required excavation} = \frac{\text{refuse volume}}{\text{assumed in place density of earth}}$$

$$\text{Hours for excavation} = \frac{\text{required excavation}}{\text{machine excavation rate}}$$

Spreading:

Given: solid wastes average 400 lb/cu yd off the packer truck when emptied at the sanitary landfill.

$$\text{Volume of refuse to be spread} = \frac{\text{refuse volume}}{400\ \text{lb/cu yd}}$$

$$\text{Hours for spreading} = \frac{\text{volume of refuse to be spread}}{\text{machine compacting rate}}$$

Table 4-9. Physical Productivity Coefficients for Sanitary Landfill Equipment, Indiana, 1970[1]

Machine Class[5]	Assumed Density (lb/cu yd)	Excavation Capacity[2] (bcy/hr)[4]	Spreading Capacity[3] (lcy/hr)[4]	Compacting Capacity[3] (lcy/hr)[4]
1	1000	56	1200	855
2	1000	76	1200	855
3	950	110	1200	1275
4	800	210	1128	775
5	1000	260	2300	885
6	1000	400	2430	1290
7	1000	560	3000	1440
8	1100	650	4200	1600
9	1300	260	2760	2916
10	–	300	–	–

1. All coefficients are given at 100 percent of efficiency (although the equipment is more likely to be operated at 50 percent of true efficiency in practice).

2. Excavation coefficients assume a 100-foot one-way push as would be the case when the trench method of sanitary landfilling is used.

3. Spreading and compacting coefficients assume a 100-foot one-way push with three to four passes required.

4. Notation:

    bcy = banked cubic yard
    lcy = loose cubic yard

5. Examples of the machines included in the respective classes are presented in Table 4-7.

Source: The estimated coefficients have been provided by Whayne Supply Company (Caterpillar equipment dealer), Louisville, Kentucky.

Compacting:

Volume of refuse to be spread = volume of refuse to be compacted

$$\text{Hours for compacting} = \frac{\text{volume of refuse to be compacted}}{\text{machine compacting rate}}$$

Given the time requirement and the hourly owning and operating cost estimate, the daily or annual (250 working days per year) cost of operating each piece of equipment at various disposal volumes can be calculated. The proper machine or combination of machines for each volume of solid wastes is then selected on a least-cost basis. The disposal system's equipment expense is thus the minimum result when the costs of several machines and combinations of machines are compared.

In functional form this total annual equipment expense appears as follows:

$$C_E^D = E_F + E_V(V)$$

where: C_E^D = the total annual cost of equipment at a sanitary landfill

E_F = the total annual fixed cost of equipment at a sanitary landfill
E_V = the total annual variable cost of equipment at a sanitary landfill
V = the daily volume of solid wastes in tons.

It should be noted that total annual fixed cost (E_F in the function) is invariant to volume but does change approximately with shifts in the least-cost equipment that is employed. While it is usually the case that fixed cost is directly dependent upon the equipment that is used, a different result is obtained in this study. Specifically, the fixed cost of equipment consists entirely of the eight hour labor requirement and does not include such expenses as depreciation and interest. This approach is the result of the latter costs being developed on an hourly basis which, in turn, makes them dependent upon volume. Since labor requirements coincide between machines in one or two cases, it therefore follows that fixed cost will aproximately reflect equipment usage.

The specific least-cost expressions of total annual equipment expense are presented in Appendix A according to volume. The total annual cost and average annual cost per ton of solid wastes disposal, as provided by these expressions, are summarized in Table 4-10.

Personnel

The wages and salaries of the personnel required at a sanitary landfill contribute significantly to the total costs of such an operation. As will be noted, there is a difference in these requirements between county and regional sanitary landfills. The cost of equipment operators is included in the equipment owning and operating cost estimates and is, therefore, excluded from the present discussion.

A fee of some type is often charged for use of the sanitary landfill. At county operations this necessitates the provision of a *fee-collector*. The wage rate for such a position is assumed to be $3 per hour, plus fringe benefits of twenty-five percent, or $3.75 per hour in total.

When the disposal operation is regional in scope the need for a fee-collector is eliminated. *A scaleman* is employed whose duties can include the collection of user fees in addition to the operation of the scale. The wage rate for this position is assumed to be $4 per hour, including fringe benefits.

A *foreman* is required to coordinate and oversee the operation of a

Table 4-10. Estimated Annual Equipment Owning and Operating Expense, Indiana, 1970

Volume (tons/day)	Machine Class Required[1]	Total Annual Cost	Annual Cost per Ton	Volume (tons/day)	Machine Class Required[1]	Total Annual Cost	Annual Cost per Ton
25	4	$15068	$2.411	875	9 & 10	$ 57758	$0.264
50	5	16325	1.306	900	9 & 10	59147	0.263
75	5	18815	1.003	925	9 & 10	60488	0.262
100	5	20173	0.807	950	9 & 10	61504	0.259
125	5	21488	0.688	975	9 & 10	62839	0.258
150	5	23109	0.616	1000	9 & 10	64217	0.257
175	6	24479	0.560	1025	9 & 10	65381	0.255
200	6	26340	0.527	1050	9 & 10	66573	0.254
225	6	27860	0.495	1075	9 & 10	67766	0.252
250	9	29388	0.470	1100	9 & 10	69084	0.251
275	9	30668	0.446	1125	9 & 10	70421	0.250
300	9	32233	0.430	1150	9 & 10	71771	0.2496
325	9	33556	0.413	1175	9 & 10	73356	0.2497
350	9	34918	0.399	1200	6 & 9	82967	0.2770
375	9	36294	0.387	1225	7 & 9	83930	0.2741
400	9	37540	0.375	1250	7 & 9	85644	0.2740
425	9	39022	0.367	1275	7 & 9	87254	0.2737
450	9	41495	0.369	1300	7 & 9	88825	0.2733
475	9	43916	0.370	1325	7 & 9	90258	0.2725
500	9 & 10	45299	0.362	1350	7 & 9	91694	0.2717
525	9 & 10	45705	0.348	1375	7 & 9	93081	0.2708
550	9 & 10	46312	0.337	1400	7 & 9	94500	0.2699
575	9 & 10	46868	0.326	1425	7 & 9	95625	0.2684
600	9 & 10	47674	0.318	1450	7 & 9	97066	0.2678
625	9 & 10	48455	0.310	1475	7 & 9	98611	0.2674
650	9 & 10	49374	0.304	1500	7 & 9	100263	0.2673
675	9 & 10	50280	0.298	1525	7 & 9	101832	0.2671
700	9 & 10	50824	0.290	1550	7 & 9	103624	0.2674
725	9 & 10	51330	0.283	1575	7 & 9	105340	0.2675
750	9 & 10	52174	0.278	1600	7 & 9	107130	0.2678
775	9 & 10	53005	0.274	1625	8 & 9	116096	0.2858
800	9 & 10	54022	0.270	1650	8 & 9	117556	0.2850
825	9 & 10	55337	0.268	1675	8 & 9	118804	0.2837
850	9 & 10	56641	0.267	1700	8 & 9	120490	0.2835

1. Examples of the machines included in the respective classes are presented in Table 4-7.

sanitary landfill at both the county and regional levels. In the case of smaller operations, those with volumes of less than 250 tons per day, the equipment operator can serve as foreman in addition to the operation of his machine. (At a volume of 225 tons per day, for example, the class 6 machinery operator needs only 4.9 hours to fulfill his machine-hour duties, and thus has 3.1 hours of an eight hour work day to provide for the management function.) As volumes increase beyond 250 tons per day, however, it becomes unreasonable to expect the machinery operator to effectively manage the sanitary landfill. At these levels of operation, a foreman is employed specifically to perform the management function. The salary, including fringe benefits, for the foreman position is assumed to be $12,500 per year.

In most cases, a sanitary landfill will also require the services of at least one *laborer*. This employee is needed to remove blown papers from fencing, refuel machinery, provide landscape maintenance, and perform other general maintenance functions. It is assumed, however, that such a position is necessary only at medium to larger county and regional sanitary landfills. One laborer will thus be employed when volumes of disposal range from 250 to 499 tons per day. When volumes exceed 500 tons per day, it is assumed that two laborers are required. The wage rate for each laborer is $2.50 per hour including fringe benefits.

As in most businesses, it is essential that proper records of the sanitary landfill operation be kept. This is especially true in the case of regional disposal operations, as the collection and dissemination of information is basic to the success of the cooperative effort. A *secretary* is required to provide this information function. The need for a secretary is assumed to exist when volumes reach and exceed 250 tons per day. The wage rate for a secretary is taken as $2.75 per hour, including fringe benefits.

It is assumed that a sanitary landfill is open to the public from 8:00 A.M. to 6:00 P.M., five days per week. Total annual wages of hourly personnel are based on such a ten hour day (with the exception of the secretarial position which entails an eight hour day). Personnel requirements (excluding machinery operators) and the resulting annual costs are presented in Table 4-11 for county and regional sanitary landfills.

Table 4-11. Personnel Requirements and Annual Costs for County and Regional Sanitary Landfills, Indiana, 1970[1]

Volume (tons/ day)	Total Annual Cost		Fee Collec- tor[2]	Foreman	Laborer	Scaleman[3]	Secretary
	County	Regional					
0–249	$ 9750	$10400	$9750			$10400	
250–499	34470	35120	9750	$12500	$ 6500	10400	$5720
500–1700	40970	41620	9750	12500	13000	10400	5720

1. Personnel requirements exclude machinery operators.
2. A fee collector is employed only at a county sanitary landfill.
3. A scaleman is employed only at a regional sanitary landfill.

Annual Site Maintenance and Development

Periodic maintenance must be performed in order for a sanitary landfill to function properly. Repairs and preventive maintenance are necessary to insure the continued usefulness of the scale, scalehouse, equipment shed, and other facilities. In addition to specific site preparation requirements, this expense also provides for the application of the final two-foot cover of earth to completed trenches. The Des Moines study indicates that this cost is approximately equal to ten percent of the initial site development expense.[5]

Administration and Overhead

Expenditures must be made for utility services, heating oil, office supplies, and other such administrative and overhead requirements. Contingency funds to meet unexpected expenses are also included in this category. A representative annual cost of $10 per ton of daily volume is assumed.

Total Cost

The total annual cost of operating a sanitary landfill includes those expenses as noted above: (1) planning and designing costs, (2) initial site development costs, (3) land expense, (4) the owning and operating expense of equipment, (5) wages and salaries of personnel, (6) annual site maintenance and development costs, and (7) an administration and overhead expense. These cost components can be combined to provide a mathematical expression of total annual cost that assumes the general form:

$$C^D = C_F^D + C_V^D(V)$$

where: C^D = the total annual disposal cost at a sanitary landfill
C_F^D = the total annual fixed cost at a sanitary landfill
$C_V^D(V)$ = the total annual variable cost at a sanitary landfill
V = the daily volume of solid wastes in tons

The specific values of this total annual cost expression are provided in Appendix B (Tables B-1 and B-2), according to county and regional sanitary landfills, respectively.

The fixed part of the total annual cost (C_F^D in the general expression) is representative of the fixed plant that is required at the various volumes of solid wastes disposal. Over the range of volumes considered in this study— from 0 to 1700 tons per day—there are seven such sizes of fixed plant (see

Appendix B). The implication of this result, from an economic standpoint, is that there exist seven short-run cost curves.[6] The costs as developed in this study can thus be thought of as estimates, at twenty-five ton increments, of points on such short-run cost curves. If the estimates are considered as samples of the costs that are represented by the respective short-run cost curves, they can be regressed on daily volume to provide short-run predictive expressions of total annual cost at a sanitary landfill. These expressions are presented in Tables 4-12 and 4-13 for county and regional operations, respectively. The total and average annual costs that result from these expressions are depicted graphically in Figures 4-1 and 4-2.

In the short-run, as implied by the results above, the operating range of any given sanitary landfill is restricted according to the fixed plant that is available. In the long-run, however, all factors of production become variable; the equipment at existing sanitary landfills will wear out and require replacement or entirely new sanitary landfills can be brought into operation. On the

Table 4-12.   Predictive Expressions for Short-Run Total Annual Cost at a County Sanitary Landfill, Indiana, 1970

Daily Volume (tons)		Predictive Expression[1]		
0–199	$c_{C_1}^D$ =	\$34408.55 + 106.758 (V) (828.842) (7.413)		R^2 = 0.977 n = 7
200–249	$c_{C_2}^D$ =	\$32187.07 + 123.482 (V) (1281.153) (6.027)		R^2 = 0.998 n = 3(2)
250–499	$c_{C_3}^D$ =	\$56251.18 + 124.354 (V) (931.477) (2.521)		R^2 = 0.997 n = 10
500–999	$c_{C_4}^D$ =	\$76055.84 + 99.735 (V) (917.374) (1.221)		R^2 = 0.997 n = 20
1000–1199	$c_{C_5}^D$ =	\$64120.18 + 114.621 (V) (1075.332) (0.987)		R^2 = 0.999 n = 8
1200–1624	$c_{C_6}^D$ =	\$57151.43 + 126.764 (V) (3701.565) (2.634)		R^2 = 0.994 n = 17
1625–1700	$c_{C_7}^D$ =	\$77443.47 + 118.590 (V) (4698.472) (2.826)		R^2 = 0.999 n = 4

1. Where: c_C^D = the total annual short-run cost at a county sanitary landfill
V = the daily volume of solid wastes in tons
( ) = the standard error of the estimate
n = the number of observations in the sample.

2. Note: a special cost estimate has been made at a volume of 212 tons per day. This additional information is necessary to provide sufficient degrees of freedom for a significant estimate of the short-run total annual cost curve for volumes ranging from 200 to 249 tons per day.

Table 4-13. Predictive Expressions for Short-Run Total Annual Cost at a Regional Sanitary Landfill, Indiana, 1970

Daily Volume (tons)	Predictive Expression[1]		
0–199	$c_{R_1}^D$ =	\$38800.27 + 119.615 (V) (273.340) (2.445)	$R^2 = 0.998$ $n = 7$
200–249	$c_{R_2}^D$ =	\$38293.07 + 123.482 (V) (1281.153) (6.027)	$R^2 = 0.998$ $n = 32$
250–499	$c_{R_3}^D$ =	\$62353.42 + 124.359 (V) (933.076) (2.525)	$R^2 = 0.997$ $n = 10$
500–999	$c_{R_4}^D$ =	\$82148.03 + 99.751 (V) (917.347) (1.221)	$R^2 = 0.997$ $n = 20$
1000–1199	$c_{R_5}^D$ =	\$70226.18 + 114.621 (V) (1075.332) (0.987)	$R^2 = 0.999$ $n = 8$
1200–1624	$c_{R_6}^D$ =	\$69099.62 + 122.432 (V) (880.534) (0.627)	$R^2 = 0.999$ $n = 17$
1625–1700	$c_{R_7}^D$ =	\$83549.47 + 118.590 (V) (4698.472) (2.826)	$R^2 = 0.999$ $n = 4$

1. Where: c_R^D = the total annual short-run cost at a regional sanitary landfill
    V = the daily volume of solid wastes in tons
    ( ) = the standard error of the estimate
    n = the number of observations in the sample

2. Note: a special cost estimate was made at a volume of 212 tons per day. This additional information was necessary to provide sufficient degrees of freedom for a significant estimate of the short-run total annual cost curve for volumes ranging from 200 to 249 tons per day.

basis of expected volume, then, a choice must be made as to the most desirable level of fixed plant. To facilitate this decision, it is an advantage to have a long-run planning function. Such a planning function relates cost to volume over as wide a range of operation as is relevant for planning purposes. The theoretical and empirically acceptable approach to the derivation of such a long-run average cost function requires that the minimum cost point on each of the respective short-run average cost curves be used to form an envelope of short-run minimum average cost points. It is this envelope of short-run costs, then, that constitutes the long-run average cost curve; any one of the least-cost short-run operating situations can be adopted in the long-run. [7,8]

As indicated in Figures 4-1 and 4-2, however, none of the short-run average cost curves as developed in this study reaches a minimum. In some cases a fixed plant is replaced by a lower cost fixed plant before the minimum average cost is reached. In other instances, the constraint of a twelve hour work day is reached before the full effect of decreasing cost is realized. The generally ac-

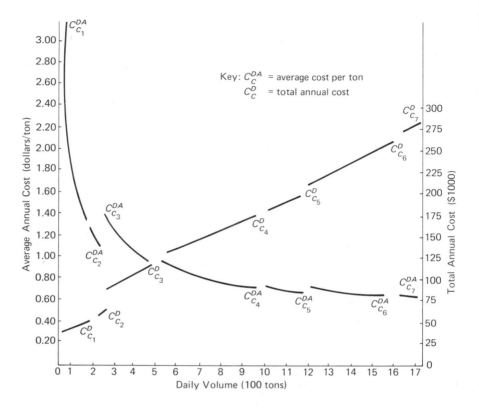

Figure 4-1. Estimated Short-Run Total and Average Annual Disposal Cost at a County Sanitary Landfill, Indiana, 1970

cepted approach to the derivation of long-run average cost is thus inapplicable for the data under consideration.

An alternative approach is to make use of the fact that synthesized disposal cost data is being used in this study. That is, the total annual cost estimates as developed previously are least-cost by construction for each particular volume. The regression of the appropriate total cost estimates on the range of volumes up to 1700 tons per day, thus provides long-run cost expressions for county and regional disposal operations.[9] In an attempt to formulate the best possible long-run expressions, linear, quadratic, and cubic models can be fitted to the data. All three forms give a good fit, but the cubic form seems to provide a closer approximation at the smaller volumes, and is thus chosen for both the county and regional expressions.

The long-run planning curve for county sanitary landfills is of the form: [10]

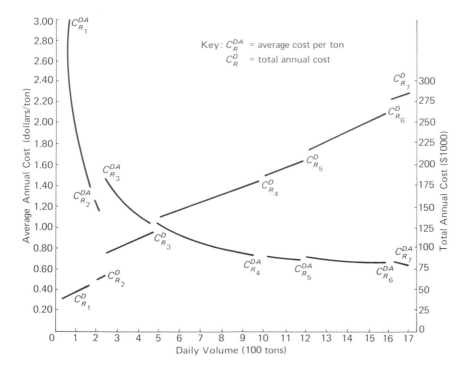

Figure 4-2. Estimated Short-Run Total and Average Annual Disposal Cost at a Regional Sanitary Landfill, Indiana, 1970

$$C_C^{DA} = \$1.016 + \frac{89.986}{(V)} - 0.0006\,(\,V\,) + 0.0000002\,(\,V\,)^2$$

where: C_C^{DA} = the average annual per ton cost of disposal at a county sanitary landfill in the long-run

V = the daily volume of solid wastes in tons.

The cost estimates resulting from this long-run expression for average cost at a county sanitary landfill are depicted graphically in Figure 4-3.

The long-run planning expression for regional sanitary landfills is of the form: [11]

$$C_R^{DA} = \$1.024 + \frac{112.043}{(V)} - 0.0006\,(\,V\,) + 0.0000002\,(\,V\,)^2$$

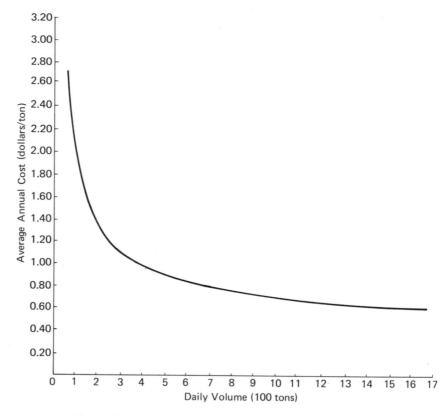

Figure 4-3. Estimated Long-Run Average Annual Disposal Cost at a County Sanitary Landfill, Indiana, 1970

where: C_R^{DA} = the average annual per ton cost of disposal at a regional sanitary landfill in the long-run

      V = the daily volume of solid wastes in tons

The results of this expression are as indicated in Figure 4-4.

SUMMARY

A solid wastes disposal system consists of three operations: storage, collection, and disposal. The total cost of the system must include the costs of each of these activities. In the case of disposal site location decisions, however, only the collection and disposal costs need be considered.

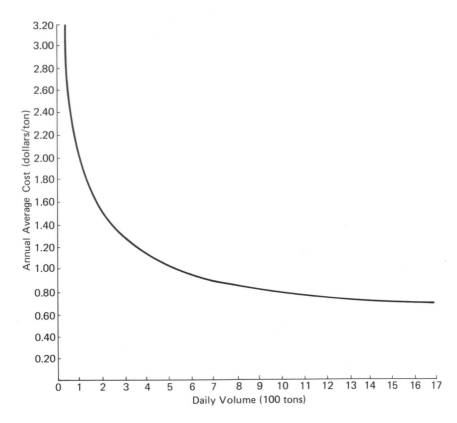

Figure 4–4. Estimated Long-Run Average Annual Disposal Cost at a Regional Sanitary Landfill, Indiana, 1970

Collection costs consist of the expenses for equipment and personnel. These equipment and personnel requirements differ between rural and urban collection systems, so that separate collection cost functions must be developed for urban and rural areas. The total annual cost of a rural collection system is given by:

$$C_R^C = \$7849.30 + 718.224\,(H)$$

where: C_R^C = the total annual cost for a given rural collection system
    H = the number of hours required to complete the collection along the system's routes per collection.

The total annual cost of an urban collection system (off-route collection transport to the disposal site) is provided by:

$$C_U^C = \$6470.00 + 10.706 \, (H)$$

where: C_U^C = the total annual cost for a given urban collection system

H = the number of hours required per year for off-route transport of solid wastes to and from a disposal site.

Solid wastes disposal is assumed to take place at a sanitary landfill. The trench method of sanitary landfilling is assumed. The costs of the sanitary landfill method of disposal include: (1) planning and designing costs, (2) initial site development costs, (3) land expense, (4) equipment owning and operating expense, (5) wages and salaries of personnel, (6) annual site maintenance and development costs, and (7) administration and overhead expense.

The initial site development and personnel requirements differ between county and regional sanitary landfills. Such differences are reflected in the respective costs of these two levels of organization. Separate long-run planning functions are thus derived for county and regional sanitary landfills. The county planning curve is of the form:

$$C_C^{DA} = \$1.016 + \frac{89.986}{(V)} - 0.0006 \, (V) + 0.0000002 \, (V)^2$$

where: C_C^{DA} = the average annual per ton cost of disposal at a county sanitary landfill in the long-run

V = the daily volume of solid wastes in tons.

The long-run planning expression for regional sanitary landfills is of the form:

$$C_R^{DA} = \$1.024 + \frac{112.043}{(V)} - 0.0006 \, (V) + 0.0000002 \, (V)^2$$

where: C_R^{DA} = the average annual per ton cost of disposal at a regional sanitary landfill in the long-run

V = the daily volume of solid wastes in tons.

NOTES

1. R.M. Alexander, G.D. Smith, and J.V. Walters, *Chilton County Solid Waste Disposal Demonstration Project Detailed Progress Report*, Environmental Protection Agency, Bureau of Solid Waste Management, Division of Demonstration Operations, 1971.

2. *Ibid.* Estimates are in the form of monthly time series data for the period January 1969 to May 1971. Data has been adjusted to reflect June 1970 dollars through the use of the Wholesale Price Index.

3. *Clean and Green (Chilton County, Alabama)*, A Solid Waste Disposal Demonstration Project, Department of Health, Education and Welfare, Public Health Service, Bureau of Solid Waste Management, 1970.

4. Henningson, Durham & Richardson, Inc., *Collection and Disposal of Solid Waste for the Des Moines Metropolitan Area*, U.S. Department of Health, Education and Welfare, Public Health Service, Environmental Control Administration, Solid Wastes Program, Cincinnati, 1968.

5. Henningson, Durham & Richardson, Inc., *op. cit.*, pp. 4-28.

6. The short-run is defined as that period of production which is of such a length that at least one of the inputs is in fixed supply.

7. D.S. Watson, *Price Theory and Its Uses*, Houghton Mifflin Company, New York, 1963.

8. For empirical examples, see A. Lin and E.O. Heady, "Empirical Cost Functions for Labour-Intensive Paddy Farms in Formosa," *The Australian Journal of Agricultural Economics*, Vol. 14: No. 2, pp. 138-149, and J. Johnston, *Statistical Cost Analysis*, McGraw-Hill Book Company, Inc., New York, 1960.

9. Johnston, *op. cit.*, pp. 64-71.

10. The county planning curve is obtained from the total annual long-run cost function for a county sanitary landfill:

$$C_C^D = \$22496.59 + 253.888(V) - 0.147(V)^2 + 0.00005(V)^3 \quad R^2 = 0.995$$
$$\quad\quad (2438.354)\ (12.266) \quad\quad (0.0165) \quad\quad (0.000006) \quad\quad n = 69$$

where: C_C^D = the total annual long-run cost of disposal at a county sanitary landfill

V = the daily volume of solid wastes in tons

$(\ )$ = the standard error of the estimate

n = the number of observations in the sample

11. The regional planning curve is obtained from the total annual long-run function for a regional sanitary landfill:

$$C_R^D = \$28010.87 + 255.920(V) - 0.148(V)^2 + 0.00005(V)^3 \quad R^2 = 0.996$$
$$\quad\quad (2426.447)\ (12.155) \quad\quad (0.0163) \quad\quad (0.000006) \quad\quad n = 69$$

where: C_R^D = the total annual long-run cost of disposal at a regional sanitary landfill

V = the daily volume of solid wastes in tons

( ) = the standard error of the estimate

n = the number of observations in the sample

Chapter Five

The Economic Feasibility of a Regional Solid Wastes System

The costs of collection and disposal have been established as the determinants of the least-cost number and location of solid wastes disposal sites. As such, these costs provide the basis for the analytical framework used in this study. The purpose of this chapter is to introduce empirical evidence into this analytical framework, and thereby provide some indication as to the economic feasibility of a regional solid wastes system for the Southwestern Indiana and Kentucky Council of Governments region.

REVIEW OF METHODOLOGY

The analytical framework used to evaluate the economic feasibility of a regional solid wastes system has been considered in detail in a previous chapter.[1] A brief review is undertaken in this section, however, to provide a more substantive basis for the presentation of the empirical results.

The approach that is taken to the formulation of disposal site location decisions has been adapted from Stollsteimer.[2] The objective of this procedure—to determine the least-cost size, number, and location of solid wastes disposal sites—is accomplished by minimizing the objective function (the combined costs of collection and disposal).

Three steps are required in the minimization of the objective function with respect to disposal site numbers and locational patterns. As a first step, a collection cost function that has been minimized for varying numbers and locations of disposal sites must be obtained.

Once the least-cost transportation patterns have been established, the resulting solid wastes volumes that are to be directed to each of the sanitary landfills can be determined. The second step, then, is to calculate the disposal costs that correspond with these volumes.

75

Finally, the alternative solid wastes systems can be compared on the basis of their respective combined collection and disposal costs. This third step establishes the identity of the least-cost system and provides for the evaluation of the economic feasibility of a regional solid wastes system.

COLLECTION PATTERNS AND COSTS

The development of a collection cost function that has been minimized for varying numbers and locations of disposal sites is the first step in the determination of the least-cost solid wastes system for the Southwestern Indiana and Kentucky Council of Governments region. The basic assumptions that are made concerning solid wastes collection include: (1) collection is the responsibility of the individual counties and the city of Evansville; (2) collection is not undertaken at the regional level; and (3) collected solid wastes are always routed to the nearest sanitary landfill. The general parameters upon which collection is structured are presented in Table 5-1.

Collection patterns are established by the Noonan-Whinston routing algorithm so as to be of minimum cost for each of the alternative solid wastes systems.[3] (A description of these disposal systems is provided in Table 5-2.) From an operational standpoint, the Noonan-Whinston algorithm starts by selecting a collection point on the perimeter of the collection points to be serviced. A collection vehicle, originating at the disposal site, is routed to this initial

Table 5-1. General Collection Routing Parameters, Southwestern Indiana and Kentucky Council of Governments Region, Indiana, 1971

County	Time of Longest Route[1]	Average Time per Collection Point (minutes)	Collection Vehicles		Average Maximum Driving Speed (mph)
			Number[2]	Capacity (tons)	
Gibson	480	4.2	10	6	35
Pike	480	4.8	10	6	35
Posey	480	5.4	10	6	35
Spencer	480	5.6	10	6	35
Vanderburgh	480	9.4	10	6	35
Warrick	480	6.6	10	6	35
City of Evansville	480	160	40	3.5	35

1. A target constraint that can be exceeded when necessary.
2. An arbitrarily specified fleet size that can be exceeded or less than fully utilized as necessary.

Table 5-2. Description of Solid Wastes Disposal Systems, Southwestern Indiana and Kentucky Council of Governments Region, Indiana, 1971 [1]

Disposal System [2]	Type	Scope	Sanitary Landfill Site Number(s)
1	Single	County	1
2	Single	County	2
3	Single	County	3
4	Single	County	4
5	Dual	County	5, 6
6	Dual	County	7, 8
7	Single	Regional	1
8	Single	Regional	2
9	Single	Regional	3
10	Single	Regional	4
11	Single	Regional	5
12	Dual	Regional	6, 7
13	Dual	Regional	8, 9
14	Dual	Regional	10, 11
15	Triple	Regional	12, 13, 14
16	Triple	Regional	15, 16, 17

1. See Table 3-3 and Figures 3-8 through 3-13, and Table 3-4 and Figure 3-14, for detailed location information on the county and regional sanitary landfills, respectively.

2. Disposal System 4 exists only for Warrick County.

collection point and then to the next closest collection point. This process of routing by measure of closest association is continued within the constraints of an eight hour work day and the load limit of the collection vehicle. If a full load is realized prior to the eight hour time constraint, the collection vehicle is returned to the disposal site for emptying, and then sent back out to continue servicing collection points until eight hours of collection are achieved. The total time required for rural collection is then provided on the basis of each optimal routing design. An example of these results for one particular system is contained in Appendix C.

Solid wastes collection service is not assumed to be provided by the counties for the incorporated cities and towns within their respective borders. The influence of the solid wastes collected in these municipalities is of importance, however, and must be recognized in the analysis. The "off-route" collection time that is required for the transport of these solid wastes to appropriate disposal sites is thus calculated.[4] The parameters assumed in the estimation of such off-route time requirements are the same as those specified for the city of Evansville in Table 5-1.

The rural and urban times corresponding with the alternative solid wastes systems, can then be combined and used with the appropriate collection cost functions, to determine the total annual cost of collection for each system. The collection cost functions as developed previously are: [5]

$$C_R^C = \$7849.30 + 718.224\,(H)$$

where: C_R^C = the total annual cost for a *rural* collection system

H = the number of hours required per collection,

and for urban collection:

$$C_U^C = \$6470.00 + 10.706\,(H)$$

where: C_U^C = the total annual cost of "off-route" travel for an *urban* collection system

H = the number of hours required per year for off-route travel to and from the disposal site.

The estimated total annual cost of collection for each of the alternative solid wastes systems is provided by county in the tables in Appendix D. These are the minimized costs for varying numbers and locations of sanitary landfills.

THE COST OF DISPOSAL

The total annual cost of disposal for each of the alternative solid wastes systems must be calculated as the second step in the determination of the least-cost solid wastes system. The assumed method of solid wastes disposal is the sanitary landfill.

Due to certain personnel and equipment differences, separate disposal cost functions are relevant for county and regional sanitary landfill operations. The total annual cost for disposal at a county sanitary landfill is given by: [6]

$$C_C^D = \$22496.59 + 253.888\,(V) - 0.147\,(V)^2 + 0.00005\,(V)^3$$

where: C_C^D = the total annual cost for disposal at a county sanitary landfill

V = the daily volume of solid wastes in tons.

The annual cost per ton for disposal at a regional sanitary landfill is calculated according to: [7]

$$C_R^{DA} = \$1.024 + \frac{112.043}{(V)} - 0.0006\ (V) + 0.0000002\ (V)^2$$

where: C_R^{DA} = the annual cost per ton for disposal at a regional sanitary land-fill

V = the daily volume of solid wastes in tons.

This average cost, when multiplied by the annual volume of solid wastes from a given county, provides the total annual cost to that county for the disposal of its solid wastes at a particular regional sanitary landfill. [8]

The estimated total annual cost of disposal for each of the alternative solid wastes systems is presented by county in the tables in Appendix E. These are the minimized costs of disposal for varying numbers and locations of disposal sites.

TOTAL COST OF THE SOLID WASTES SYSTEMS

The third and final step in the evaluation of the economic feasibility of a regional solid wastes system requires that the minimized costs of collection and disposal be combined for each of the alternative systems. The total costs that result for the alternative systems are presented in Appendix F.

An examination of these cost totals reveals that for every county, the least-cost county system is a single-site system. In the cases of Gibson, Posey, Vanderburgh, and Warrick counties, moreover, there is at least one regional solid wastes system that incurs a lower total cost than does the least-cost county system. Pike and Spencer counties and the city of Evansville, on the other hand, are seen to incur a loss from their respective least-cost regional systems. These results are summarized in Table 5-3.

A regional system is not unique to an individual county, however. It is a cooperative effort involving several participants. The least-cost system to the region is the one with the least collective cost. The least-cost regional system need not be the same for both an individual county and for the region as a whole.

In order to determine which of the regional solid wastes systems is of least-cost, it is first necessary to compute the grand total cost for each of these systems. This grand total cost is obtained by summing the individual county costs for each particular regional system. A comparison of the grand total costs is provided in Table 5-4. As indicated, System 15 incurs the least

Table 5-3.   The Least-Cost County and Regional Solid Wastes Systems, Southwestern Indiana and Kentucky Council of Governments Region, Indiana, 1971

County	Least-Cost County System		Least-Cost Regional System		Net Savings with Least-Cost Regional System
	System Number	Total Cost	System Number	Total Cost	
Gibson	2	$ 216119	8	$ 206466	+$9653
Pike	1	150817	9	150909	−92
Posey	2	180727	14	169224	+11503
Spencer	2	181087	13	185154	−4067
Vanderburgh	2	123291	7	98856	+24435
Warrick	3	187385	13	157743	+29642
City of Evansville	3	1913980	15	1965529	−51549

Table 5-4.   Grand Total Annual Costs for Alternative Regional Solid Wastes Systems, Southwestern Indiana and Kentucky Council of Governments Region, Indiana, 1971

Disposal System	Grand Total Annual Cost (dollars)	Disposal System	Grand Total Annual Cost (dollars)
7	3166988.83	12	3203277.22
8	3164849.61	13	3144082.90
9	3264325.93	14	3194672.06
10	3309529.42	15*	3011224.42
11	3116816.96	16	3119333.40

*The least-cost regional solid wastes system.

collective cost. It is thus System 15, with three sites located as shown in Figure 5-1, that is selected as the least-cost regional system.

The economic feasibility of regional System 15 is evaluated on the basis of the total net savings that it provides to the region. As indicated in Table 5-5, all participants except Gibson County realize positive disposal savings at the regional sanitary landfills. These savings represent the economies to scale that are gained by the regional over the county disposal operations. The costs of collection for regional System 15 are found to be considerably higher than they are for the individual county systems and negative savings are incurred. The total added cost when regional System 15 is selected over the individual county sys-

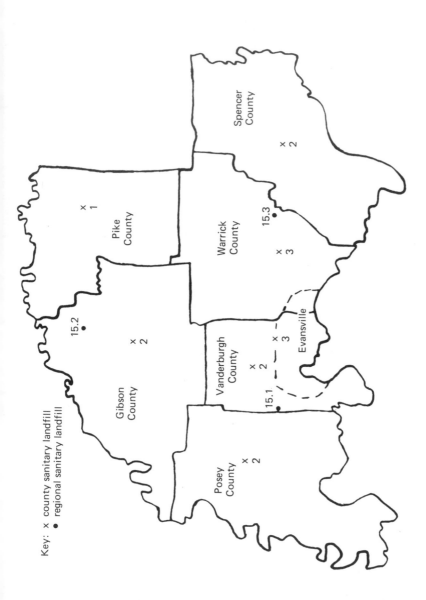

Figure 5–1. Least-Cost Sanitary Landfill Site Locations, By County and for the Southwestern Indiana and Kentucky Council of Governments Region, Indiana, 1971

Table 5-5. Total Net Saving of the Least-Cost Regional Solid Wastes System, Southwestern Indiana and Kentucky Council of Governments Region, Indiana, 1971

County	Annual Collection Saving (dollars)	Annual Disposal Saving (dollars)	Annual Net Saving (dollars)
Gibson	− 9032	− 1547	−10579
Pike	− 20487	+ 14045	− 6442
Posey	− 20347	+ 26358	+ 6011
Spencer	− 18506	+ 8356	−10150
Vanderburgh	− 1379	+ 24845	+23466
Warrick	− 15924	+ 8188	− 7736
City of Evansville	− 81770	+ 30221	−51548
Total	−166815	+110466	−56349

tems is $56,349 per year. The disposal economies of the regional system which amount to $110,466 per year are outweighed by the increase in collection costs which total $166,815. On the basis of this estimate, it must be concluded that a six county regional solid wastes system is not economically feasible.

Closer examination of Table 5-5 reveals that the primary cause for the increased cost of the regional system is the increased transportation cost incurred by Evansville. Such a result is not totally unexpected, however, given the original formulation of the problem. The regional sanitary landfill that is closest to the city of Evansville is located at a point some fifteen miles to the northwest of the city center (disposal Site 15.1 in Figure 5-1). This placement of the regional disposal site must be compared to the least-cost county sanitary landfill located at a point four miles to the north of the metropolitan center (see Figure 5-1). The negative collection savings that result from the adoption of the regional system are only logical, therefore, given this distance differential.

The increased collection costs ($81,770) that are incurred by Evansville are of such a magnitude that they cannot be offset by the disposal economies ($30,221) that are realized with the regional system. These disposal economies, moreover, are somewhat limited since the solid wastes from Evansville constitute such a large proportion of the total at the regional sanitary landfill. The additional solid wastes from the counties are not sufficient to cause significant decreases in the average cost of regional disposal.

The increased costs incurred by Gibson, Pike, Spencer, and Warrick counties are also a result of the greater distances to the regional sanitary landfills of System 15 (see Table 5-5). In the case of Gibson and Warrick counties, as noted in Figure 5-1, each has a regional disposal site located within its borders.

These sites are not centrally located however, so that the haul distances required by the respective least-cost county systems will be shorter than those required by the regional system.

The economies to scale at the regional sanitary landfills in Gibson and Warrick counties are insufficient to offset the increased collection costs of the regional solid wastes system. The regional disposal site in Gibson County, moreover, is seen to incur diseconomies. This unexpected result indicates that the average cost of disposal is higher at the regional sanitary landfill than it is at Gibson County's least-cost county disposal site. Such a situation arises because of the relatively small volume of solid wastes disposed of at the regional site in Gibson County. That is, a regional sanitary landfill involves a larger number of fixed and variable inputs than does a county sanitary landfill. When a regional site receives only slightly greater quantities than a county site, it is quite possible that the cost at the regional site will be greater than at the county site.

The counties of Pike and Spencer are required, under System 15, to deliver their solid wastes to the regional disposal sites located in Gibson and Warrick counties, respectively (see Figure 5-1). This is clearly a more expensive collection operation than is required by the least-cost county systems. Again, the disposal savings of the regional systems are not sufficient to offset the increased collection costs.

An annual net saving is realized by Posey and Vanderburgh counties when regional System 15 is adopted. As seen in Table 5-5, significant disposal economies are gained by both counties as their solid wastes are deposited at the same regional sanitary landfill that is used by the city of Evansville. These disposal savings are of sufficient magnitude to more than offset the increased collection costs of the regional system. In the case of Vanderburgh County, the net saving from regional System 15 is made even more attractive by the limited loss that is incurred for collection.

ALTERNATIVE REGIONAL FORMULATIONS

It was established in the preceding section that a regional solid wastes system is not an economically feasible alternative for the Southwestern Indiana and Kentucky Council of Governments region. Given certain modifications, however, the economic feasibility of the regional system might be improved. In particular, it is only necessary that an overall positive net saving be realized by the region. If the total net saving is positive, some of the participants can continue with a loss, but be subsidized by those who gain, so that everyone benefits from the regional solid wastes system.

Additional Regional Disposal Systems

A primary source of inefficiency in the regional system as originally formulated is the collection of solid wastes by the city of Evansville. The hauling of collected solid wastes to a regional sanitary landfill located fifteen miles away is considerably less efficient than is transport to a local sanitary landfill located only four miles from the city. One possible modification, therefore, is to include additional regional systems with sanitary landfills at locations closer to Evansville. Systems 1000 and 1001 are thus established with single disposal sites located at approximately five and ten miles, respectively, from the city of Evansville. In addition to expected collection cost savings, these new regional systems, each with a single sanitary landfill, should also provide maximum economies of disposal.

Under this new formulation, the total annual cost for the county systems remains unchanged. A comparison of the grand total costs with the new regional systems included reveal that System 1000, at a distance of five miles from Evansville, is the least-cost regional solid wastes system (see Figure 5-2).

The economic efficiency of System 1000 as compared to the least-cost county systems is analyzed in Table 5-6. As indicated, the collection savings remain negative for all participants, with the total loss increased by $119,458 over the original situation (compare to Table 5-5). Disposal savings continue to be positive and are increased as the economies to scale at the single regional disposal site are realized. The total net savings from System 1000 are still negative. Even with disposal site location adjustment, then, a regional solid wastes system is found to be economically infeasible.

A closer review of Table 5-6 indicates that the collection loss for Evansville has, in fact, been reduced with System 1000. The negative collection savings that result from this regional system are reduced by some $15,088 from the original situation. Increased disposal economies ($12,879) are also realized with the single disposal site of System 1000. The reduced collection loss and increased disposal economies are insufficient, however, to provide a positive net saving to Evansville.

Vanderburgh County also realizes collection cost savings when regional System 1000 is adopted. As depicted in Figure 5-2, the sanitary landfill of System 1000 is more centrally located in Vanderburgh County than was disposal Site 15.1. Collection cost savings for Vanderburgh County, although still negative, are thus significantly improved by System 1000, as is indicated in Table 5-6 (compare to Table 5-5). These collection cost savings are augmented by the increased disposal economies at the single regional sanitary landfill of System 1000. The net result of these collection and disposal cost savings is a positive net saving for Vanderburgh County when regional System 1000 is adopted.

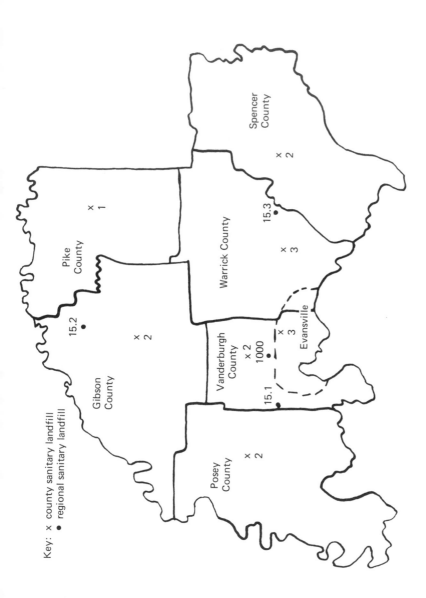

Figure 5-2. Least-Cost Sanitary Landfill Site Locations, By County and for the Southwestern Indiana and Kentucky Council of Governments Region (with Additional Systems), Indiana, 1971

Table 5-6.   Total Net Saving of the Least-Cost Regional Solid
Wastes System (with Additional Regional Systems), Southwestern
Indiana and Kentucky Council of Governments Region,
Indiana, 1971

County	Annual Collection Saving (dollars)	Annual Disposal Saving (dollars)	Annual Net Saving (dollars)
Gibson	− 79986	+ 29839	−50147
Pike	− 52220	+ 25714	−26506
Posey	− 24930	+ 27979	+ 3049
Spencer	− 57743	+ 26692	−31051
Vanderburgh	− 517	+ 25728	+25211
Warrick	− 18264	+ 30283	+12019
City of Evansville	− 66682	+ 43100	−23582
Total	−300342	+209335	−91007

In contrast to the preceding results, the counties of Gibson, Pike, Posey, Spencer, and Warrick are forced to incur increased collection cost losses ($72,091 over the original) when System 1000 is instituted. As can be seen in Figure 5-2, the replacement of disposal Sites 15.1, 15.2, and 15.3 by the single site of System 1000 causes an increase in the total distances and, thus, total costs for transporting the solid wastes collected in these counties. Even with increased disposal economies, the increased collection costs faced by Gibson, Pike, and Spencer counties under System 1000 cannot be offset. The net savings to these three counties are negative. Sufficient disposal savings are realized by the counties of Posey and Warrick, on the other hand, to counter the increased collection costs. These two counties have positive net savings (see Table 5-6).

Exclude the City of Evansville

Another alternative for improving the economic feasibility of the regional solid wastes system might be to modify the region so as to exclude the city of Evansville. All other participants remain the same as before. With this formulation, each of the least-cost county systems continues to have a single sanitary landfill. The minimum cost regional system becomes System 11 with a single disposal site located in Gibson County (see Figure 5-3).

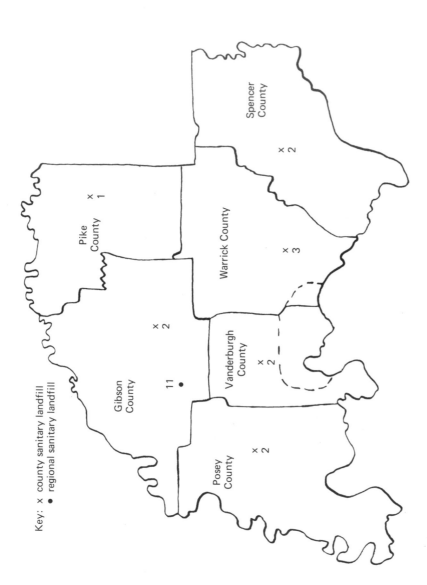

Figure 5-3. Least-Cost Sanitary Landfill Site Locations, By County and for the Southwestern Indiana and Kentucky Council of Governments Region (Excluding Evansville), Indiana, 1971

Table 5-7.   Total Net Saving of the Least-Cost Regional Solid Wastes System (Excluding Evansville), Southwestern Indiana and Kentucky Council of Governments Region, Indiana, 1971

County	Annual Collection Saving (dollars)	Annual Disposal Saving (dollars)	Annual Net Saving (dollars)
Gibson	− 73508	+ 24846	−48662
Pike	− 37269	+ 23840	−13429
Posey	− 21213	+ 24679	+ 3466
Spencer	− 51515	+ 24079	−27436
Vanderburgh	− 6895	+ 25917	+19022
Warrick	− 18950	+ 20866	+ 1916
Total	−209350	+144227	−65123

The economic feasibility of this alternative is considered in Table 5-7. As indicated, there is a significant increase in the collection cost for all participants. This result is expected given the single regional sanitary landfill and the increased transport distances that are required with System 11.

Disposal savings are realized by all participants in this regional system. Even in the absence of Evansville, the quantity of solid wastes for disposal is sufficient to yield substantial savings. In fact, these disposal savings are greater than when Evansville is included; this system has a single sanitary landfill site whereas the original system has three sites.

Without Evansville, however, only Posey, Vanderburgh, and Warrick counties benefit from a regional solid wastes system (see Table 5-7). The total net savings to the region under regional System 11 is a negative $65,123 per year. The exclusion of Evansville is thus not a sufficient modification to make the regional solid wastes system economically feasible.

Subregional Systems

Each of the alternative regional formulations considered thus far has continued to yield negative total savings. The primary cause for these negative results has been the cost of collection in a region that covers approximately 3000 square miles. A further alternative exists, therefore, to limit this collection cost loss: reduce the size of the region. That is, create subregions with only two or three participating counties.

One such subregion is suggested by the previous results. With each of the alternative regional formulations considered thus far, the counties of Posey and Vanderburgh (excluding the city of Evansville) have realized positive net savings. These two counties can be combined to form a subregion with a single regional sanitary landfill located on their common border (see Figure 5-4).

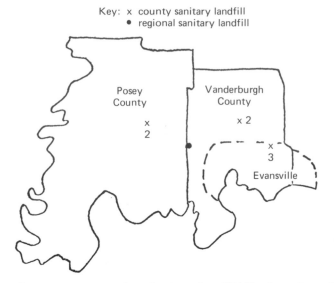

Key: x county sanitary landfill
• regional sanitary landfill

Figure 5–4. Least-Cost Sanitary Landfill Site Locations, By County and for the Posey County-Vanderburgh County-Evansville Subregion, Indiana, 1971

The results of this subregional system are presented in Table 5-8. As indicated, Vanderburgh County benefits considerably from this association. Posey County, however, suffers a net loss as increased collection costs more than offset the economies to scale at the regional sanitary landfill. This subregional system is found to be economically infeasible.

Another possible subregional system would include the counties of Posey and Vanderburgh and the city of Evansville (see Figure 5-4). Evansville is included in this system to increase the volume and, thus, cause greater disposal economies at the regional sanitary landfill. The savings that are realized with this

Table 5-8. Total Net Savings of the Regional Solid Wastes System (Posey and Vanderburgh Counties Subregion), Southwestern Indiana and Kentucky Council of Governments Region, Indiana, 1971

County	*Annual Collection Saving (dollars)*	*Annual Disposal Saving (dollars)*	*Annual Net Saving (dollars)*
Posey	−21187	+ 3218	−17969
Vanderburgh	− 1379	+12255	+10876
Total	−22566	+15473	− 7093

subregional system are indicated in Table 5-9. As expected, significant disposal economies are gained by the counties of Posey and Vanderburgh. The net savings of these counties from the subregional system are insufficient, however, to offset the increased collection cost to Evansville. Once again, the subregional system is not economically feasible.

The analysis of this latter subregional system can be extended some-what further. Suppose that the city of Evansville is in a position where it has no choice as to the location of its sanitary landfill. All possible sites within the city limits have been exhausted. Potential sanitary landfill sites are available only in the surrounding counties. (This is apparently the situation that Evansville will be facing in the not too distant future.) The counties, then, will no doubt provide a major input into the location decision. In fact, this decision quite likely will be made for the city. There will be no question of least-cost location from the city's standpoint.

Now, suppose that this city disposal site is also designated the site for the subregional sanitary landfill. Its location will be such that this is not totally unreasonable. The city would therefore experience no collection cost differential between the local and subregional systems. A positive disposal saving for the city would be likely, moreover, as it combines with Posey and Vander-burgh counties in a larger-scale disposal operation.

The economics of this arrangement are summarized in Table 5-10. All three participants are seen to enjoy a net positive saving. The total system is economically feasible.

Residential Solid Wastes Only

It is also of interest to observe that with smaller volumes (such as those represented by residential solid wastes) a regional solid wastes system

Table 5-9. Total Net Saving of the Regional Solid Wastes System (Posey and Vanderburgh Counties and City of Evansville Subregion), Southwestern Indiana and Kentucky Council of Governments Region, Indiana, 1971

County	Annual Collection Saving (dollars)	Annual Disposal Saving (dollars)	Annual Net Saving (dollars)
Posey	− 24929	+26095	+ 1166
Vanderburgh	− 517	+24702	+24185
City of Evansville	− 81770	+ 5868	−75902
Total	−107216	+56665	−50551

Table 5-10. Total Net Saving of the Regional Solid Wastes System (Posey and Vanderburgh Counties and City of Evansville Modified Subregion), Southwestern Indiana and Kentucky Council of Governments Region, Indiana, 1971

County	Annual Collection Saving (dollars)	Annual Disposal Saving (dollars)	Annual Net Saving (dollars)
Posey	−24929	+26095	+ 1166
Vanderburgh	− 517	+24702	+24185
City of Evansville	−	+ 5868	+ 5868
Total	−25446	+56665	+31219

becomes economically feasible. Consider, for example, the contiguous counties of Posey and Vanderburgh. If the same subregional system is adopted as was presented above, however, with only residential solid wastes, a total net saving of $9,687 per year is realized (see Table 5-11). The disposal economies at the regional sanitary landfill become especially significant, since the county disposal operations are forced by the small volumes to operate on the steepest section of their average cost curves. Moreover, the increased collection cost due to the regional system is kept to a minimum by the mutually acceptable location of the regional sanitary landfill.

A REVISED REGIONAL SYSTEM

As originally formulated, the regional solid wastes system was found to be economically infeasible. Increased costs for the collection activity were less than offset by the savings realized at the regional disposal facility.

Table 5-11. Total Net Saving of the Regional Solid Wastes System (Posey and Vanderburgh Counties Subregion with Only Residential Solid Wastes), Southwestern Indiana and Kentucky Council of Governments Region, Indiana, 1971

County	Annual Collection Saving (dollars)	Annual Disposal Saving (dollars)	Annual Net Saving (dollars)
Posey	−3708	+ 1557	− 2151
Vanderburgh	− 230	+13068	+12838
Total	−3938	+14625	+ 9687

Subsequent modifications to this system yielded certain insights which can be used to develop a revised system. It was observed, for instance, that the presence of a large metropolitan area tended to dominate the region. Consequently, the most feasible system was always the one with a sanitary landfill located closest to Evansville. When an attempt was made to exclude the city from the system, however, it met with failure, as the magnitude of the overall disposal savings was seriously diminished.

An apparent impasse had been reached: include Evansville in the regional system and its collection cost would contribute heavily to the system's infeasibility; exclude the city and lose the disposal economies necessary for feasibility. It was then suggested that this problem could be surmounted if the city landfill site was also designated a regional site. Such a situation could arise in practice, particularly when the city exhausts all possible sites within its borders. There would no longer be a collection cost differential for the city. A positive disposal saving would be possible, however, as Evansville combined with one or more counties for the common disposal of their solid wastes.

One final assumption is now introduced. Ordinary collection-route packer trucks of the type considered thus far are not necessarily the least-cost method for transporting solid wastes. This is particularly true where longer hauls are involved. Instead, larger capacity trucks carrying more highly-compacted loads can be used. A transfer station is constructed for the purpose of transferring the locally-collected wastes into a larger vehicle for transport to a regional sanitary landfill.[9] The cost for the transfer station and the haul cost to the disposal site are assumed to total $13.50 per hour.[10]

The System

A revised regional system is now proposed. It will still include the original counties of Gibson, Pike, Posey, Spencer, Vanderburgh, and Warrick and the city of Evansville. The individual county systems remain as before. It is assumed under this new system, however, that Evansville is forced to seek a sanitary landfill site out in Vanderburgh County. The county dictates its placement. The location of this disposal site for Evansville is such that it might also serve as a regional site.

Each of the counties, with the exception of Vanderburgh, is assumed to transport its solid wastes to the regional disposal site via a transfer station. The transfer station for each county is located where the least-cost county sanitary landfill would be in the respective local systems. Because the regional site is located in Vanderburgh County no transfer station is assumed. A transfer station would also be required for Evansville, but since there will be no difference in transportation cost between the local and regional systems, the cost for this facility is left unconsidered (see Figure 5-5).

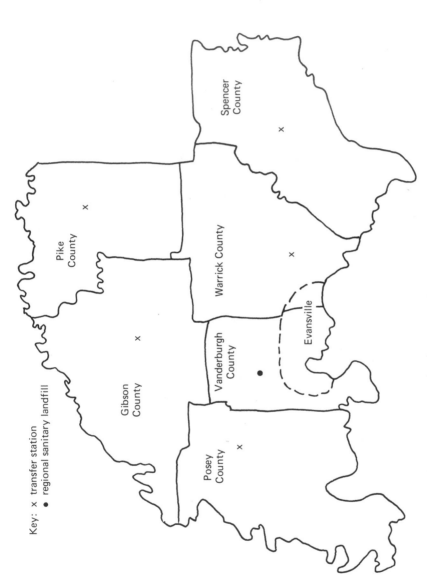

Figure 5-5. Least-Cost Regional Sanitary Landfill Site Location, Southwestern Indiana and Kentucky Council of Governments Region (Revised Regional System), Indiana, 1971

Economic Feasibility

The economic potential for the system just described is analyzed in Table 5-12. Collection losses are incurred by Gibson, Pike, Posey, Spencer, and Warrick counties as might be expected. The regional sanitary landfill is assumed to be located sufficiently close to the least-cost local site for Vanderburgh County to leave that county's collection cost unaffected.[11] Similarly, the city of Evansville experiences no difference in its collection cost. Disposal savings are realized at the single regional sanitary landfill by all participants. Overall, the system is seen to provide a small, but positive, net saving. It is economically feasible.

It should be recognized that Evansville and Vanderburgh County are the big individual gainers from the regional system. Most of the rural counties enjoy disposal savings but their transportation costs more than offset these savings. Quite obviously, some type of pricing scheme is needed to transfer the benefits to all participants. Each member would have to receive a net saving if the system were to become operational.

Finally, the $46,000 net savings represents some two to three percent of the total annual system cost. Given the estimating procedures, this would indicate that the regional system should be able to operate for at least the same total cost as the several individual county systems. Further reductions in the cost of a regional system are contingent upon greater savings in transportation cost. In the present analysis, it will be noted that the regional system has a concentration of solid wastes being generated on one side of the region. The specification of a region with a metropolitan area near its geographic center should tend to reduce transportation costs and thereby increase the likelihood of an economically feasible regional system.

Table 5-12.   Total Net Saving of the Revised Regional Solid Wastes System, Southwestern Indiana and Kentucky Council of Governments Region, Indiana, 1971

County	Annual Collection Saving (dollars)	Annual Disposal Saving (dollars)	Annual Net Saving (dollars)
Gibson	− 36450	+ 29839	− 6611
Pike	− 30834	+ 25715	− 5119
Posey	− 23382	+ 27979	+ 4597
Spencer	− 35856	+ 26692	− 9164
Vanderburgh	−	+ 25727	+25727
Warrick	− 36693	+ 30283	− 6410
City of Evansville	−	+ 43101	+43101
Total	−163215	+209336	+46121

SUMMARY

The costs of collection and disposal have been established as the principal determinants of a solid wastes disposal site location decision. As such, these costs
provide the basis for the analytical framework that is used in this book.

Empirical evidence has been developed in this chapter and introduced into the analytical framework with the aim of determining if a regional
solid wastes system is, in fact, the least-cost alternative for the Southwestern
Indiana and Kentucky Council of Governments region. These results when expressed in terms of the stated objectives of this study indicate that:

(1) The least-cost county solid wastes system for each county in the
Southwestern Indiana and Kentucky Council of Governments region has a single
sanitary landfill. The specific system numbers and total annual costs of these
least-cost county systems are contained in Table 5-3.

(2) The least-cost regional solid wastes system for the Southwestern
Indiana and Kentucky Council of Governments region is System 15 which has
three sanitary landfills. The total annual cost of this system if allocated on a per
ton basis to each of the participating counties and Evansville is provided in
Tables F-1 to F-7 in Appendix F.

(3) As initially formulated, the least-cost solid wastes system for the
Southwestern Indiana and Kentucky Council of Governments region is the several individual county systems. This conclusion is based on the collective loss that
is realized by the counties when the least-cost regional system is adopted instead
of the least-cost county systems (see Table 5-5).

Several alternative formulations of the regional system were also
considered in an effort to determine if an economically feasible system existed.
These modified formulations and their respective results suggest:

(1) An alternative regional system, with a landfill located closer to
Evansville, reduces the loss incurred under the original formulation, but still
results in higher costs than do the original county systems.

(2) Excluding Evansville from the region does not improve the economic feasibility of the regional system.

(3) A subregional system consisting of Posey and Vanderburgh counties is economically infeasible, as the increased collection costs of the system are
not offset by increased economies to scale at the regional sanitary landfill.

(4) A subregional system consisting of Posey and Vanderburgh counties and the city of Evansville is also economically infeasible. In this case, the
addition of Evansville creates disposal economies for Posey and Vanderburgh
counties, but not to the extent that is necessary to offset the increased collection costs of the regional system.

(5) A subregional system which includes the city of Evansville, in addition to Posey and Vanderburgh counties, can be economically feasible if the city's sanitary landfill site is made to coincide with the subregional site.

(6) When the collection and disposal of only residential solid wastes (that is, a small volume) is considered, a regional solid wastes system also becomes economically feasible.

Finally, these modifications indicate that a revised regional system that is economically feasible can be developed. Characteristics of such a system include: (1) the original counties and the city of Evansville participate, (2) county systems remain unchanged, (3) the city of Evansville must accept a sanitary landfill site located in Vanderburgh County, (4) each of the counties (except Vanderburgh) uses a transfer station and large-scale transport equipment, and (5) the city sanitary landfill is located such that it can also serve as the regional sanitary landfill. The net positive savings offered by this system are evidence of its economic feasibility. In order for it to become operational, however, a differential pricing scheme would be needed to guarantee each political unit a net benefit and thereby encourage participation.

NOTES

1. See Chapter 2, "Methodology," for the full presentation of the analytical framework.

2. J.F. Stollsteimer, "A Working Model for Plant Numbers and Locations," *Journal of Farm Economics*, Vol. 45: No. 3, pp. 631-645.

3. R. Noonan and A. Whinston, "An Information System for Vehicle Scheduling," *Software Age*, December 1969, pp. 8-13.

4. Off-route collection time requirements are also calculated for the city of Evansville. In this case, however, the Noonan-Whinston algorithm is used first to estimate the total collection time per route. The average delay time per load (160 minutes) is then subtracted from the total time to provide the off-route collection transport time. This approach is adopted rather than selecting a single point from which to calculate off-route time due to the larger geographic area of Evansville. Also, a more realistic approximation of collection vehicle requirements can be made if this approach is followed for Evansville.

5. See Chapter 4, "Synthesis of Cost Data," for the development of these collection cost functions.

6. See Chapter 4, "Synthesis of Cost Data," for the development of this disposal cost function.

7. *Ibid.*

8. Other methods of cost allocation among counties are possible and could be considered, but are beyond the scope of this study.

9. Transfer stations could, of course, be used within a county, too. This is not assumed to be the case in this study.

10. This cost is based on a transfer vehicle with a 15 ton or 75 cubic yard capacity. Transfer cost information is taken from L. Haug, "When Does Transfer Pay Off?," *Refuse Removal Journal*, Vol. 19: No. 8, pp. 52-54.

11. It could have been further assumed that Vanderburgh County and the city of Evansville have a combined disposal operation at the former's least-cost sanitary landfill. Disposal savings for the regional system would be reduced in this case but the system would still be economically feasible.

Chapter Six

Conclusions

The Southwestern Indiana and Kentucky Council of Governments region is faced with a solid wastes management problem. Much of the solid wastes currently generated in this region is either burned or disposed of in open dumps, publically operated and otherwise, and in illegal roadside dumping areas. The existence of these disposal practices is a violation of state environmental criteria.

It was the purpose of this study to determine the appropriate replacement for ongoing methods of solid wastes disposal. Such a decision was to be based on economic feasibility, given that environmental standards were satisfied. The objective was to minimize cost. Economic theory suggested that a regional approach might prove optimal.

The same general selection procedure was applied for each of several alternative disposal systems. A least-cost system was developed individually for each of the counties, for the city of Evansville, and for the Southwestern Indiana and Kentucky Council of Governments region as a whole. Once established, these least-cost systems were compared in terms of total dollar costs to determine the disposal system that was, in fact, the least-cost alternative.

General

The empirical findings of this study indicate that a regional solid wastes system can be a least-cost alternative if sufficiently well-defined. That is, the addition of certain assumptions concerning, for instance, the placement and use of a city's sanitary landfill and inclusion of transfer stations is necessary to obtain such a result. While these specifications do tend to cloud somewhat any general implications, the meaning of this solution for at least the case in point is clear. If the several members of the Southwestern Indiana and Kentucky Council of Governments join forces in a common disposal system, it will provide them with a collective least-cost means for the provision of this service. As compared to individual systems, an average annual net saving of some twelve cents per ton of solid waste handled can be expected.[1]

Disposal and Collection Costs

Economic feasibility of a regional solid wastes system is extremely dependent upon the costs for collection and disposal. The increased collection cost inherent in regional systems must be more than offset by increased disposal economies.

The shape of the average cost curve for disposal at a sanitary landfill suggests that those counties with the smallest volumes of solid wastes should generally realize the greatest cost savings from regional disposal. Both the original and revised regional disposal systems tend to indicate that such a relationship does hold. These results are summarized in Table 6-1. The revised regional system, with a single regional sanitary landfill, follows this pattern exactly. The original system, with its optimal design of three disposal sites, shows this same definite trend.

Generalizations on collection loss due to regional systems are more difficult. Volume and distance have an interrelated effect. There was some slight indication that collection loss tends to diminish as the volume of the county increases. This probably reflects the bias in locating sanitary landfills so as to minimize distance from larger concentrations of solid waste.

Table 6-1. Annual Per Ton Disposal Saving for Selected Regional Solid Wastes Systems, Southwestern Indiana and Kentucky Council of Governments Region, Indiana, 1971

County	*Inverse Rank by Volume*[1]	*Annual Disposal Saving per Ton*	
		Original System[2]	*Revised System*[3]
Gibson	6	−$0.039	$0.748
Pike	2	0.959	1.756
Posey	4	0.984	1.044
Spencer	3	0.419	1.340
Vanderburgh	1	2.132	2.207
Warrick	5	0.247	0.914
City of Evansville	7	0.127	0.182

1. Volume is in tons per day of solid wastes; ranked inversely by volume.

2. Original system is the initial regional system formulated in this study.

3. Revised system is the last proposed system with Evansville's sanitary landfill serving as either a local or regional site and transfer stations for local collection transport.

County Results

While the focus of this study has been on the economic feasibility of regional solid wastes systems, the importance of the least-cost results for local systems should not be overlooked. In Indiana, as elsewhere around the country, the consolidation of public services in rural areas, under relatively more economic units such as the county, will be no small achievement. Such cooperation is becoming evermore important, however, as the demand for public services increases.

Alternative single and double-site systems were evaluated in this study for each of the counties. In every case, a single sanitary landfill was the least-cost approach. Any rural county with plans for more than one disposal site within its solid wastes system should quite likely reconsider the economics of the situation.

Metropolitan Domination

In the case of the study region and, possibly, for other regions of similar size and composition, the presence of a large city such as Evansville tends to dominate and dictate the actions that may be taken by the region as a whole. This domination results from the high volume of solid wastes generated within the metropolitan area; Evansville produces nearly twice as much solid wastes as does the rest of the region combined. Collection costs are extremely important to the city due to the large volume involved, and far outweigh the disposal economies that are realized at a regional sanitary landfill. The solid wastes system that is least costly to the city is thus the one with the closest disposal site, be it city or regional. Because of its influence, moreover, the system that is optimal for the city is also least-cost to the region.

Any attempt to exclude Evansville from the region is found to be economically infeasible. As originally formulated, a regional solid wastes system is found to be too expensive with Evansville in the region, but also too expensive without Evansville.

It is also of interest to note that in the absence of Evansville, a single-site regional system becomes least-cost, while with Evansville included, a triple-site system is the least expensive. This result again attests to the influence of the city, as the three site system offers the closest sanitary landfill.

In order for a regional solid wastes system to be economically feasible the costs of collection must be held to a minimum. Consequently, the city of Evansville's collection cost must be minimized also. The addition of regional sanitary landfills in closer proximity to Evansville is found to reduce that city's collection cost but, in so doing, increases the distances and collection costs to the other members of the region. Adjustment of the regional disposal site location is thus insufficient to establish the economic feasibility of a regional solid wastes system.

It becomes apparent that a more detailed specification of the regional system is needed if the necessary assimilation of the metropolitan area into the system is to be accomplished. That is, it must be assumed that the city has exhausted its stock of disposal sites. Moreover, the site for a city sanitary landfill in one of the surrounding counties is determined by that county. This may be underestimating the bargaining power of the metropolitan area, but it does not seem totally unrealistic. The location of the city's new sanitary landfill is then assumed to be sufficiently central to permit its use as a regional site if economically feasible. Imposition of additional restrictions such as these appears to be necessary when a metropolitan area dominates a region as Evansville does.

Transfer Stations

The inclusion of transfer stations as a means for reducing collection cost within a regional system also deserves further comment. Many communities, in Indiana and elsewhere, have included such facilities in their solid wastes systems when disposal must be performed at a site several miles away. There is a definite economic appeal for a system that transfers collected solid wastes to a larger vehicle for transport in a more highly compacted form at a lower per unit cost. The analogy for regional systems seems clear.

The importance of transfer stations in a regional system is indicated in the results of this study. Such facilities were assumed in the revised regional formulation. In contrast, the modified system with disposal site 1000 did not include transfer stations. Both of these systems featured single regional sanitary landfills; they were located similarly in the region. A comparison is provided in Table 6-2. In nearly every case the collection cost for the regional system was reduced by the inclusion of a transfer station. The revised system could be improved somewhat more if a transfer station was not included for Warrick County.

Subregional Systems

The region under consideration suggests two types of subregional systems: (1) those that exclude Evansville and (2) those that include this metropolitan area.

Analysis in this study indicates that in the absence of Evansville disposal economies are insufficient to offset increased collection costs. Even though collection costs are held down by a mutually acceptable disposal site, they cause the subregional system to be economically infeasible. Quite possibly transfer stations could be used to advantage.

Table 6-2. Reduction in Collection Cost due to Transfer Stations, Southwestern Indiana and Kentucky Council of Governments Region, Indiana, 1971

| | *Annual Collection Cost per Ton*[1] | | |
County	*System 1000*[2] *(no transfer station)*	*Revised System*[3] *(transfer station)*	*Reduction*
Gibson	$2.029	$0.925	$1.104
Pike	3.556	2.100	1.456
Posey	0.928	0.870	0.058
Spencer	2.890	1.795	1.095
Vanderburgh	0.044	–	–
Warrick	0.550	1.104	-0.554
City of Evansville	0.280	–	–

1. Annual collection cost for a regional system given in dollars per ton of solid wastes transported to the disposal site.
2. System 1000 is a modification of the original regional system with a regional sanitary landfill located at a point closer to the city of Evansville.
3. Revised system includes a common local-regional disposal site for Evansville and transfer stations.

Assumptions made concerning Evansville's disposal site affect the feasibility of subregional systems in the presence of this metropolitan area. Only when the subregional disposal site is made coincidental with the city's is such a system economically feasible.

These results should not be taken for more than they are. The analysis was limited to two subregions, each of which was chosen rather subjectively. Additional subregions need to be evaluated before any definite generalizations can be made.

LIMITATIONS AND NEEDS FOR FURTHER RESEARCH

It should be noted that the analytical framework used in this study is not intended to predict actual cost conditions under more specific circumstances. It is intended primarily as a decision-making tool. The cost estimates that it provides may have practical significance but are of real importance in a relative sense to one another.[2]

In its present form, the model that has been developed requires considerable manual calculation. To insure the feasibility of the study, therefore, it was necessary to impose certain restrictions upon the analysis. One such adjustment was required in the selection of potential sanitary landfill sites. It would have been ideal if a larger number of sites could have been selected throughout the region, and if all possible combinations of sites could have been evaluated within a county and for the region as a whole. This was not possible given the nature of the model.

It was also not possible to follow an iterative procedure in the calculation of the collection and disposal costs. That is, in the case of multidisposal site systems, the initial allocation of solid wastes was not improved upon so that the marginal costs of collection and disposal were equal between sites. As single-site systems were found to be least-cost at the county level, this shortcoming had no effect. The original regional system, however, had three disposal sites. These results are thus somewhat inflated. It does not appear, in general, that the overall analysis has been distorted.

If the framework that has been followed in this study is to be of practical value, it would be desirable that much of the computational effort be shifted to a computer. A computer adapted version of the model as used in this study would permit the consideration of a larger number of alternative solid wastes systems, allow iterative cost calculations, and, in general, provide greater flexibility for the study of system modifications.

In terms of the analysis itself, it is possible that some amount of bias has been introduced by the selection of the Southwestern Indiana and Kentucky Council of Governments region for study. This selection was made rather subjectively, primarily due to the existing political framework which makes implementation of the results a possibility. Any of several county groupings within the general area of the region could have been selected.

NOTES

1. This saving is calculated by dividing the total annual net saving of the revised regional solid wastes system (Table 5-12) by the total number of tons of solid wastes generated annually in the study region.

2. It should be specifically noted that the cost of storage has been excluded from total cost, since the storage system will not vary between regional and county solid wastes systems.

Appendix A

Least-Cost Expressions of Total Annual Sanitary Landfill Equipment Expense

Table A-1. Total Annual Least-Cost Equipment Expense at a Sanitary Landfill, Indiana, 1970

Daily Volume		Total Annual Cost
25	$10400 + 186.725 (*v*)*	$ 15068.125
50	10400 + 118.500 (*v*)	16325.000
75	10400 + 112.200 (*v*)	18815.000
100	10400 + 97.725 (*v*)	20172.500
125	10400 + 88.700 (*v*)	21487.500
150	10400 + 84.725 (*v*)	23108.750
175	10400 + 80.450 (*v*)	24478.750
200	10400 + 79.700 (*v*)	26340.000
225	10400 + 77.600 (*v*)	27860.000
250	10400 + 75.950 (*v*)	29387.500
275	10400 + 73.700 (*v*)	30667.500
300	10400 + 72.775 (*v*)	32232.500
325	10400 + 71.250 (*v*)	33556.250
350	10400 + 70.050 (*v*)	34917.500
375	10400 + 69.050 (*v*)	36293.750
400	10400 + 67.850 (*v*)	37540.000
425	10400 + 67.345 (*v*)	39021.625
450	10400 + 69.100 (*v*)	41495.000
475	10400 + 70.560 (*v*)	43916.000
500	21424 + 47.750 (*v*)	45299.000
525	21424 + 46.250 (*v*)	45705.250
550	21424 + 45.250 (*v*)	46311.500
575	21424 + 44.250 (*v*)	46867.750
600	21424 + 43.750 (*v*)	47674.000
625	21424 + 43.250 (*v*)	48455.250
650	21424 + 43.000 (*v*)	49374.000
675	21424 + 42.750 (*v*)	50280.250
700	21424 + 42.000 (*v*)	50824.000
725	21424 + 41.250 (*v*)	51330.250
750	21424 + 41.000 (*v*)	52174.000
775	21424 + 40.750 (*v*)	53005.250
800	21424 + 40.747 (*v*)	54021.600
825	21424 + 41.107 (*v*)	55337.275
850	21424 + 41.432 (*v*)	56641.200
875	21424 + 41.525 (*v*)	57758.375
900	21424 + 41.194 (*v*)	59146.600
925	21424 + 42.231 (*v*)	60487.675
950	21424 + 42.189 (*v*)	65103.550
975	21424 + 42.477 (*v*)	62839.075
1000	21424 + 42.793 (*v*)	64217.000
1025	21424 + 42.885 (*v*)	65381.125
1050	21424 + 42.999 (*v*)	66572.950
1075	21424 + 43.109 (*v*)	67766.175
1100	21424 + 43.327 (*v*)	69083.700
1125	21424 + 43.553 (*v*)	70421.125
1150	21424 + 43.780 (*v*)	71771.000
1175	21424 + 44.197 (*v*)	73355.475
1200	20800 + 51.806 (*v*)	82967.200
1225	20800 + 51.535 (*v*)	83930.375
1250	20800 + 51.875 (*v*)	85643.750
1275	20800 + 52.121 (*v*)	87254.275
1300	20800 + 52.327 (*v*)	88825.100

Table A-1. (cont.)

Daily Volume		Total Annual Cost
1325	$20800 + 52.421 (*v*)	$ 90257.825
1350	20800 + 52.514 (*v*)	91693.900
1375	20800 + 52.568 (*v*)	93081.000
1400	20800 + 52.643 (*v*)	94500.200
1425	20800 + 52.509 (*v*)	95625.325
1450	20800 + 52.597 (*v*)	97065.650
1475	20800 + 52.753 (*v*)	98610.675
1500	20800 + 52.975 (*v*).	100262.500
1525	20800 + 53.136 (*v*)	101832.400
1550	20800 + 53.435 (*v*)	103624.250
1575	20800 + 53.676 (*v*)	105339.700
1600	20800 + 53.956 (*v*)	107129.600
1625	20600 + 58.767 (*v*)	116096.375
1650	20600 + 58.761 (*v*)	117555.650
1675	20600 + 58.629 (*v*)	113803.575
1700	20600 + 58.759 (*v*)	120490.300

*v = Daily volume of solid wastes disposal in tons.

Appendix B

Total Annual Disposal Cost Expressions

Table B-1. Total Annual Disposal Cost at a County Sanitary Landfill, Indiana, 1970

Daily Volume		Total Annual Cost
25	$29525.16 + 242.809 (v)*	$ 38595.385
50	29525.16 + 174.584 (v)	38254.360
75	29525.16 + 168.284 (v)	42146.460
100	29525.16 + 153.809 (v)	44906.060
125	29525.16 + 144.784 (v)	47623.160
150	29525.16 + 140.809 (v)	50646.510
175	29525.16 + 136.534 (v)	53418.610
200	28334.00 + 142.521 (v)	56838.200
225	28334.00 + 140.421 (v)	59928.725
250	53054.00 + 138.771 (v)	87746.750
275	53054.00 + 136.521 (v)	90597.275
300	53054.00 + 135.596 (v)	93732.800
325	53054.00 + 134.071 (v)	96627.075
350	53054.00 + 132.871 (v)	99558.850
375	53054.00 + 131.871 (v)	102505.625
400	53054.00 + 130.671 (v)	105322.400
425	53054.00 + 130.166 (v)	108374.550
450	53054.00 + 131.921 (v)	112418.450
475	53054.00 + 133.381 (v)	116409.975
500	71942.00 + 110.572 (v)	127228.000
525	71942.00 + 109.071 (v)	129204.275
550	71942.00 + 108.071 (v)	131381.050
575	71942.00 + 107.071 (v)	133547.825
600	71942.00 + 106.571 (v)	135884.600
625	71942.00 + 106.071 (v)	138236.375
650	71942.00 + 105.821 (v)	140725.650
675	71942.00 + 105.571 (v)	143202.425
700	71942.00 + 104.821 (v)	145316.700
725	71942.00 + 104.071 (v)	147398.475
750	71942.00 + 103.821 (v)	149807.750
775	71942.00 + 103.571 (v)	152209.525
800	71942.00 + 103.568 (v)	154796.400
825	71942.00 + 103.928 (v)	157682.600
850	71942.00 + 104.433 (v)	160710.050
875	71942.00 + 104.346 (v)	163244.750
900	71942.00 + 104.735 (v)	166203.500
925	71942.00 + 105.052 (v)	169115.100
950	71942.00 + 105.010 (v)	171701.500
975	71942.00 + 105.298 (v)	174607.550
1000	73306.00 + 105.614 (v)	178920.000
1025	73306.00 + 105.706 (v)	181654.650
1050	73306.00 + 105.820 (v)	184417.000
1075	73306.00 + 105.930 (v)	187180.750
1100	73306.00 + 106.148 (v)	190068.800
1125	73306.00 + 106.374 (v)	192967.750
1150	73306.00 + 106.601 (v)	195897.150
1175	73306.00 + 107.018 (v)	199052.150
1200	72682.00 + 114.627 (v)	210234.400
1225	72682.00 + 114.356 (v)	212048.100
1250	72682.00 + 114.696 (v)	216052.000
1275	72682.00 + 114.942 (v)	219233.050
1300	72682.00 + 115.148 (v)	222374.400

Table B-1. (cont.)

Daily Volume		Total Annual Cost
1325	$72682.00 + 115.242 (v)$	$225377.650
1350	72682.00 + 115.335 (v)	228384.250
1375	72682.00 + 115.389 (v)	230995.708
1400	72682.00 + 115.464 (v)	234331.600
1425	72682.00 + 115.330 (v)	237027.250
1450	72682.00 + 115.418 (v)	240038.100
1475	72682.00 + 115.574 (v)	243152.650
1500	72682.00 + 115.796 (v)	246376.000
1525	72682.00 + 115.957 (v)	249516.425
1550	72682.00 + 116.256 (v)	252878.800
1575	72682.00 + 116.497 (v)	256164.775
1600	72682.00 + 116.777 (v)	264375.200
1625	72482.00 + 121.688 (v)	270225.000
1650	72482.00 + 121.582 (v)	273092.300
1675	72482.00 + 121.450 (v)	275910.750
1700	72482.00 + 121.580 (v)	279168.000

*v = Daily volume of solid wastes disposal in tons.

Table B-2.   Total Annual Disposal Cost at a Regional Sanitary
Landfill, Indiana, 1970

Daily Volume		Total Annual Cost
25	$35631.16 + 242.809 (*v*)*	$ 41701.385
50	35631.16 + 174.584 (*v*)	44360.360
75	35631.16 + 168.284 (*v*)	48252.460
100	35631.16 + 153.809 (*v*)	51012.060
125	35631.16 + 144.784 (*v*)	53729.160
150	35631.16 + 140.809 (*v*)	56752.510
175	35631.16 + 136.534 (*v*)	59524.610
200	34440.00 + 142.521 (*v*)	62944.200
225	34440.00 + 140.421 (*v*)	66034.725
250	59160.00 + 138.771 (*v*)	93852.750
275	59160.00 + 136.521 (*v*)	96703.275
300	59160.00 + 135.596 (*v*)	99838.800
325	59160.00 + 134.071 (*v*)	102733.075
350	59160.00 + 132.871 (*v*)	105664.850
375	59160.00 + 131.871 (*v*)	108611.625
400	59160.00 + 130.671 (*v*)	111428.400
425	59160.00 + 130.166 (*v*)	114480.550
450	59160.00 + 131.921 (*v*)	118524.450
475	59160.00 + 133.381 (*v*)	122515.975
500	78048.00 + 110.572 (*v*)	133334.000
525	78048.00 + 109.071 (*v*)	135310.275
550	78048.00 + 108.071 (*v*)	137487.050
575	78048.00 + 107.071 (*v*)	139613.825
600	78048.00 + 106.571 (*v*)	141990.600
625	78048.00 + 106.071 (*v*)	144342.375
650	78048.00 + 105.821 (*v*)	146831.650
675	78048.00 + 105.071 (*v*)	149308.925
700	78048.00 + 104.821 (*v*)	151422.700
725	78048.00 + 104.071 (*v*)	153499.475
750	78048.00 + 103.821 (*v*)	155913.750
775	78048.00 + 103.571 (*v*)	158315.525
800	78048.00 + 103.568 (*v*)	160902.400
825	78048.00 + 103.928 (*v*)	163788.600
850	78048.00 + 104.433 (*v*)	166816.050
875	78048.00 + 104.346 (*v*)	169350.750
900	78048.00 + 104.735 (*v*)	172309.500
925	78048.00 + 105.052 (*v*)	175221.100
950	78048.00 + 105.010 (*v*)	177807.500
975	78048.00 + 105.298 (*v*)	180713.550
1000	79412.00 + 105.614 (*v*)	185026.000
1025	79412.00 + 105.706 (*v*)	187760.650
1050	79412.00 + 105.820 (*v*)	190523.000
1075	79412.00 + 105.930 (*v*)	193286.750
1100	79412.00 + 106.148 (*v*)	196174.800
1125	79412.00 + 106.374 (*v*)	199082.750
1150	79412.00 + 106.601 (*v*)	202003.150
1175	79412.00 + 107.018 (*v*)	205158.150
1200	78788.00 + 114.627 (*v*)	216340.400
1225	78788.00 + 114.356 (*v*)	218874.100
1250	78788.00 + 114.696 (*v*)	222158.000
1275	78788.00 + 114.942 (*v*)	225339.050
1300	78788.00 + 115.148 (*v*)	228480.400

Table B-2. (cont.)

Daily Volume		Total Annual Cost
1325	$78788.00 + 115.242 (v)	$231483.650
1350	78788.00 + 115.335 (v)	234490.250
1375	78788.00 + 115.389 (v)	237447.875
1400	78788.00 + 115.464 (v)	240437.600
1425	78788.00 + 115.330 (v)	243133.250
1450	78788.00 + 115.418 (v)	246144.100
1475	78788.00 + 115.574 (v)	249259.650
1500	78788.00 + 115.796 (v)	252482.000
1525	78788.00 + 115.957 (v)	255622.425
1550	78788.00 + 116.256 (v)	258984.800
1575	78788.00 + 116.597 (v)	262428.275
1600	78788.00 + 116.777 (v)	265631.200
1625	78588.00 + 121.688 (v)	276331.000
1650	78588.00 + 121.582 (v)	279198.300
1675	78588.00 + 121.450 (v)	282016.750
1700	78588.00 + 121.580 (v)	285274.000

*v = Daily volume of solid wastes disposal in tons.

Appendix C

An Example of the Noonan-Whinston Routing Algorithm Results

The optimal routing of rural collection vehicles is determined in this study according to the Noonan-Whinston routing algorithm. An example of the results provided by this algorithm is presented in this section. System 7 of Gibson County (with a single regional sanitary landfill) has been selected for purposes of illustration.

The computer print-out from the Noonan–Whinston alogrithm begins with a list of the relevant parameters. In the example, this print-out appears as follows:

	Hr–Min
Fleet Early Start Time	0.00
Fleet Late Finish Time	8.00
Average Delay Time per Stop	0.04
Speed Modification Factor	1.00
Terminal Node Number	508

The *early and late fleet times* are seen to constrain the work day to eight hours in length. The *average delay time per stop* is interpreted as a four minute time requirement for the emptying of rural collection bins into the collection vehicle at each stop. There is no speed modification. Finally, the *terminal node number* is a code for the sanitary landfill to which the routes are directed.

The initial collection vehicle fleet that is available for routing is summarized next in the print-out. This summary is of the form:

Type	*Number*	*Capacity*
1	10	6000

where the number of collection vehicles is arbitrarily specified (and can be exceeded or less than fully utilized as necessary) and the capacity of the collection vehicles is given in thousandths of a ton.

The final preliminary in the print-out is a listing of the collection points that are to be included for scheduling. This list makes note of the solid wastes volume that must be collected at each point.

Actual routing output is provided according to the following informational categories:

Grid Number	Amount	Arrival Time
68	192	0.08
79	326	0.23
.	.	.
.	.	.
.	.	.

with the *grid number* referring to the identification of the collection point (except for Grid No. 1 which is the sanitary landfill), the *amount* indicating thousandths of a ton of solid wastes at a collection point, and *arrival time* being a cumulative record of the time required to reach each particular point (given in hours and minutes).

For the example, it was found that two days of collection would be necessary in order to service all the rural collection points in Gibson County and deposit these solid wastes at the regional sanitary landfill. The first day's routing is indicated in Table C-1 and Figure C-1. As can be seen, the total cumulative time required for this collection is 7 hours and 54 minutes. Collection for the second day is scheduled as shown in Table C-2 and Figure C-2. The time required with this routing is 8 hours and 28 minutes.

The print-out ends with a summary of the remaining collection vehicle fleet and review of the overall routing results. This overall review appears as follows:

Total Fleet Time	16.22 (hr-min)
Number of Routes	2
Number of Stops	86

Table C-1. Optimal Routing on First Day, Gibson County, Indiana, 1971

Grid Number[1]	Amount[2]	Arrival Time[3]	Grid Number[1]	Amount[2]	Arrival Time[3]
68	192	0.08	37	301	4.18
79	326	0.23	44	279	4.27
80	326	0.29	45	279	4.34
82	206	0.41	49	291	4.41
71	192	0.50	48	291	4.48
83	206	0.56	47	291	4.55
86	206	1.11	43	279	5.04
28	326	1.22	42	279	5.10
29	326	1.30	46	291	5.19
30	326	1.37	57	235	5.28
25	227	1.42	56	235	5.36
85	206	1.59	55	235	5.45
70	192	2.14	54	235	5.55
69	192	2.20	53	235	6.04
78	326	2.33	52	235	6.15
77	326	2.40	59	291	6.22
62	238	2.53	58	291	6.33
63	238	3.00	67	238	6.48
64	238	3.07	1		7.09
1		3.25	74	326	7.23
65	238	3.40	73	326	7.30
66	238	3.47	75	326	7.41
60	291	3.58	76	326	7.49
36	301	4.08			

1. Grid numbers refer to collection point numbers (except for Grid No. 1 which is the sanitary landfill).

2. Amount indicates thousandths of a ton of solid wastes at the collection point.

3. Arrival time is the cumulative time required to reach each point.

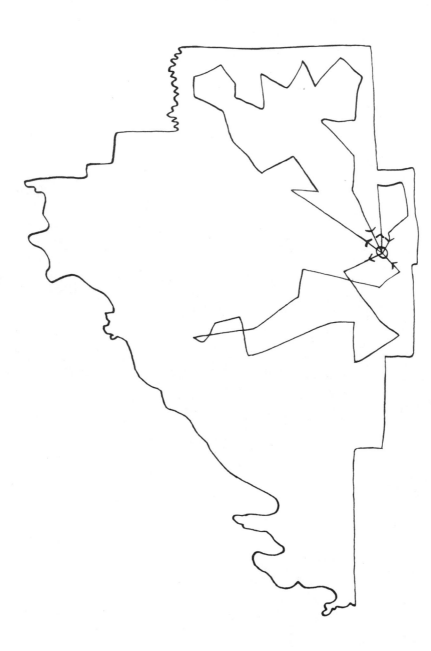

Figure C-1. Optimal Routing of Solid Wastes Collection Vehicles on the First Day, Gibson County, Indiana, 1971

Table C-2.   Optimal Routing on Second Day, Gibson County, Indiana, 1971

Grid Number[1]	Amount[2]	Arrival Time[3]	Grid Number[1]	Amount[2]	Arrival Time[3]
84	206	0.23	27	326	3.47
90	307	0.34	26	326	3.54
89	307	0.44	33	339	4.02
91	307	0.55	32	339	4.11
92	307	1.05	1		4.49
96	63	1.16	34	339	5.20
95	63	1.27	17	545	5.25
94	63	1.34	19	545	5.32
97	63	1.55	18	545	5.40
93	307	2.03	20	545	5.47
87	206	2.14	21	545	5.54
31	326	2.22	4	203	6.01
88	206	2.32	2	203	6.16
15	129	2.40	5	203	6.31
14	129	2.56	12	129	6.46
13	129	3.04	7	203	7.03
11	129	3.10	6	203	7.14
10	129	3.17	3	203	7.29
22	227	3.25	40	301	7.40
23	227	3.32	39	301	7.49
24	227	3.40	38	301	7.59

1. Grid numbers refer to collection point numbers (except for Grid No. 1 which is the sanitary landfill).

2. Amount indicates thousandths of a ton of solid wastes at the collection point.

3. Arrival time is the cumulative time required to reach each point.

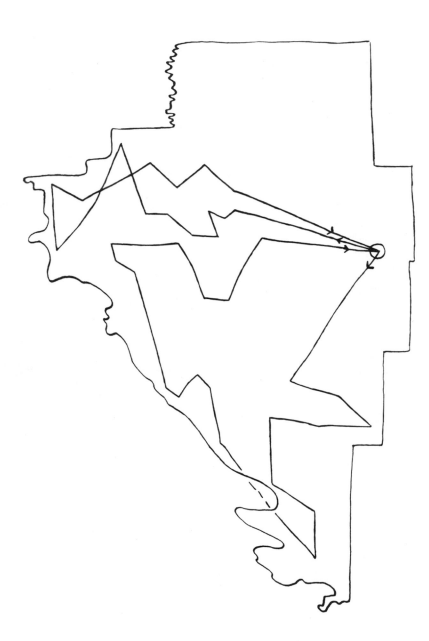

Figure C-2.   Optimal Routing of Solid Wastes Collection Vehicles on the Second Day, Gibson County, Indiana, 1971

Appendix D

Total Annual Collection Costs for the Alternative Solid Wastes Systems

Table D-1. Total Annual Collection Cost, Gibson County, Indiana, 1971

Disposal System*	Total Annual Collection Cost (dollars)	Disposal System*	Total Annual Collection Cost (dollars)
1	183,450.97	10	228,544.22
2	164,568.97	11	238,077.44
3	185,206.13	12	268,819.86
5	174,650.99	13	197,075.65
6	177,218.94	14	200,563.11
7	222,031.34	15	173,601.16
8	184,754.55	16	207,276.92
9	187,547.81		

*See Table 5–2 for a description of each system.

Table D-2. Total Annual Collection Cost, Pike County, Indiana, 1971

Disposal System*	Total Annual Collection Cost (dollars)	Disposal System*	Total Annual Collection Cost (dollars)
1	117,029.35	10	144,047.82
2	117,119.57	11	154,298.06
3	121,585.32	12	188,765.27
5	116,775.13	13	140,236.10
6	115,740.92	14	154,193.25
7	173,901.02	15	137,516.42
8	160,156.49	16	153,331.35
9	142,836.81		

*See Table 5–2 for a description of each system.

Table D-3.   Total Annual Collection Cost, Posey County, Indiana, 1971

Disposal System*	Total Annual Collection Cost (dollars)	Disposal System*	Total Annual Collection Cost (dollars)
1	138,686.86	10	177,903.95
2	137,846.70	11	159,059.73
3	139,917.61	12	166,596.89
5	135,132.56	13	169,537.12
6	145,020.57	14	153,381.03
7	160,332.25	15	159,033.87
8	173,390.45	16	197,237.30
9	187,151.99		

*See Table 5-2 for a description of each system.

Table D-4.   Total Annual Collection Cost, Spencer County, Indiana, 1971

Disposal System*	Total Annual Collection Cost (dollars)	Disposal System*	Total Annual Collection Cost (dollars)
1	150,934.32	10	199,851.13
2	143,524.31	11	195,038.57
3	148,268.20	12	195,441.28
5	129,100.91	13	173,820.18
6	136,651.57	14	164,247.27
7	221,357.09	15	162,030.26
8	232,110.74	16	167,828.05
9	218,524.59		

*See Table 5-2 for a description of each system.

Table D-5.   Total Annual Collection Cost, Vanderburgh County, Indiana, 1971

Disposal System*	Total Annual Collection Cost (dollars)	Disposal System*	Total Annual Collection Cost (dollars)
1	92,774.82	10	104,754.84
2	89,456.64	11	96,351.60
3	91,568.22	12	92,042.28
5	87,819.12	13	101,522.82
6	87,043.44	14	93,766.02
7	90,749.46	15	90,835.62
8	96,567.06	16	93,335.04
9	108,417.78		

*See Table 5-2 for a description of each system.

Table D-6. Total Annual Collection Cost, Warrick County, Indiana, 1971

Disposal System*	Total Annual Collection Cost (dollars)	Disposal System*	Total Annual Collection Cost (dollars)
1	148,043.00	9	191,500.84
2	152,311.47	10	172,372.57
3	144,003.08	11	162,953.01
4	146,621.03	12	168,932.45
5	144,747.52	13	144,085.00
6	144,688.27	14	173,516.90
7	199,415.25	15	159,927.35
8	195,711.48	16	151,970.66

*See Table 5-2 for a description of each system.

Table D-7. Total Annual Collection Cost, City of Evansville, Indiana, 1971

Disposal System*	Total Annual Collection Cost (dollars)	Disposal System*	Total Annual Collection Cost (dollars)
1	1,803,397.57	10	2,086,942.14
2	1,792,892.42	11	1,915,925.80
3	1,752,528.05	12	1,873,425.80
5	1,759,389.50	13	1,973,988.07
6	1,786,456.86	14	2,060,000.00
7	1,904,095.67	15	1,834,297.88
8	1,927,046.09	16	1,851,853.82
9	2,033,233.36		

*See Table 5-2 for a description of each system.

Appendix E

Total Annual Disposal Costs for the Alternative Solid Wastes Systems

Table E-1. Total Annual Disposal Cost, Gibson County, Indiana, 1971

Disposal System*	Total Annual Disposal Cost (dollars)	Disposal System*	Total Annual Disposal Cost (dollars)
1	51,550.33	10	21,711.39
2	51,550.33	11	21,711.39
3	51,550.33	12	39,191.43
5	74,930.11	13	50,152.98
6	78,572.74	14	26,894.66
7	21,711.39	15	53,097.13
8	21,711.39	16	61,206.97
9	21,711.39		

*See Table 5-2 for a description of each system.

Table E-2. Total Annual Disposal Cost, Pike County, Indiana, 1971

Disposal System*	Total Annual Disposal Cost (dollars)	Disposal System*	Total Annual Disposal Cost (dollars)
1	33,787.16	10	8,072.51
2	33,787.16	11	8,072.51
3	33,787.16	12	8,582.98
5	56,427.79	13	21,285.31
6	56,410.42	14	18,091.92
7	8,072.51	15	19,742.04
8	8,072.51	16	21,392.16
9	8,072.51		

*See Table 5-2 for a description of each system.

125

Table E-3.   Total Annual Disposal Cost, Posey County, Indiana, 1971

Disposal System*	Total Annual Disposal Cost (dollars)	Disposal System*	Total Annual Disposal Cost (dollars)
1	42,880.05	10	14,900.70
2	42,880.05	11	14,900.70
3	42,880.05	12	15,842.95
5	65,799.81	13	15,536.18
6	65,736.74	14	15,842.95
7	14,900.07	15	16,522.25
8	14,900.70	16	16,259.30
9	14,900.70		

*See Table 5-2 for a description of each system.

Table E-4.   Total Annual Disposal Cost, Spencer County, Indiana, 1971

Disposal System*	Total Annual Disposal Cost (dollars)	Disposal System*	Total Annual Disposal Cost (dollars)
1	37,562.32	10	10,870.19
2	37,562.32	11	10,870.19
3	37,562.32	12	23,211.06
5	60,310.00	13	11,333.78
6	60,304.46	14	24,362.02
7	10,870.19	15	29,205.66
8	10,870.19	16	30,644.36
9	10,870.19		

*See Table 5-2 for a description of each system.

Table E-5.   Total Annual Disposal Cost, Vanderburgh County, Indiana, 1971

Disposal System*	Total Annual Disposal Cost (dollars)	Disposal System*	Total Annual Disposal Cost (dollars)
1	33,834.59	10	8,107.34
2	33,834.59	11	8,107.34
3	33,834.59	12	8,620.10
5	56,450.33	13	8,453.10
6	56,336.21	14	8,620.01
7	8,107.34	15	8,989.61
8	8,107.34	16	8,846.54
9	8,107.34		

*See Table 5-2 for a description of each system.

Table E–6. Total Annual Disposal Cost, Warrick County, Indiana, 1971

Disposal System*	Total Annual Disposal Cost (dollars)	Disposal System*	Total Annual Disposal Cost (dollars)
1	43,381.88	9	13,099.11
2	43,381.88	10	13,099.11
3	43,381.88	11	13,099.11
4	43,381.88	12	27,970.46
5	66,113.60	13	13,657.75
6	66,388.93	14	29,357.42
7	13,099.11	15	35,194.23
8	13,099.11	16	29,188.55

*See Table 5–2 for a description of each system.

Table E–7. Total Annual Disposal Cost, City of Evansville, Indiana, 1971

Disposal System*	Total Annual Disposal Cost (dollars)	Disposal System*	Total Annual Disposal Cost (dollars)
1	161,452.39	10	118,351.51
2	161,452.39	11	118,351.51
3	161,452.39	12	125,835.50
5	223,146.23	13	123,398.86
6	200,653.90	14	125,835.50
7	118,351.51	15	131,230.94
8	118,351.51	16	129,142.38
9	118,351.51		

*See Table 5–2 for a description of each system.

Total Annual Costs for the Alternative Solid Wastes Systems

Table F-1. Total Annual Cost for Alternative Solid Wastes System, Gibson County, Indiana, 1971

Disposal System*	Total Annual Disposal System Cost (dollars)	Disposal System*	Total Annual Disposal System Cost (dollars)
1	235,001.30	10	250,255.61
2**	216,119.30	11	259,788.83
3	236,756.46	12	308,011.29
5	249,581.10	13	247,228.63
6	255,791.68	14	227,457.77
7	243,742.73	15	226,698.29
8	206,465.94	16	268,303.89
9	209,259.20		

*See Table 5-2 for a description of each system.
**The least-cost county solid wastes disposal system.

Table F-2. Total Annual Cost for Alternative Solid Wastes System, Pike County, Indiana, 1971

Disposal System*	Total Annual Disposal System Cost (dollars)	Disposal System*	Total Annual Disposal System Cost (dollars)
1**	150,816.51	10	152,120.33
2	150,906.73	11	162,370.57
3	155,372.48	12	197,348.25
5	173,202.92	13	161,521.41
6	172,151.34	14	172,285.17
7	181,973.53	15	157,258.46
8	168,229.00	16	174,723.51
9	150,909.32		

*See Table 5-2 for a description of each system.
**The least-cost county solid wastes disposal system.

Table F-3.   Total Annual Cost for Alternative Solid Wastes System, Posey County, Indiana, 1971

Disposal System*	Total Annual Disposal System Cost (dollars)	Disposal System*	Total Annual Disposal System Cost (dollars)
1	181,566.91	10	192,804.65
2**	180,726.75	11	173,960.43
3	182,797.66	12	182,439.84
5	200,932.37	13	185,073.30
6	210,757.31	14	169,223.98
7	175,232.95	15	175,556.12
8	188,291.15	16	213,496.60
9	202,052.69		

*See Table 5-2 for a description of each system.
**The least-cost county solid wastes disposal system.

Table F-4.   Total Annual Cost for Alternative Solid Wastes System, Spencer County, Indiana, 1971

Disposal System*	Total Annual Disposal System Cost (dollars)	Disposal System*	Total Annual Disposal System Cost (dollars)
1	188,496.64	10	210,721.32
2**	181,086.63	11	205,908.76
3	185,830.52	12	218,652.34
5	189,410.91	13	185,153.96
6	196,956.03	14	188,609.29
7	232,227.28	15	191,235.92
8	242,980.93	16	198,472.41
9	229,394.78		

*See Table 5-2 for a description of each system.
**The least cost county solid wastes disposal system.

Table F-5.   Total Annual Cost for Alternative Solid Wastes System, Vanderburgh County, Indiana, 1971

Disposal System*	Total Annual Disposal System Cost (dollars)	Disposal System*	Total Annual Disposal System Cost (dollars)
1	126,609.41	10	112,862.18
2**	123,291.23	11	104,458.94
3	125,402.81	12	100,662.29
5	144,269.45	13	109,975.92
6	143,379.65	14	102,386.03
7	98,856.80	15	99,825.23
8	104,674.40	16	102,181.58
9	116,525.12		

*See Table 5-2 for a description of each system.
**The least-cost county solid wastes disposal system.

Table F-6. Total Annual Cost for Alternative Solid Wastes System, Warrick County, Indiana, 1971

Disposal System*	Total Annual Disposal System Cost (dollars)	Disposal System*	Total Annual Disposal System Cost (dollars)
1	191,424.88	9	204,599.95
2	195,693.35	10	185,471.68
3**	187,384.96	11	176,052.12
4	190,002.91	12	196,902.91
5	210,861.12	13	157,742.75
6	211,077.20	14	202,874.32
7	212,514.36	15	195,121.58
8	208,810.59	16	181,159.21

*See Table 5-2 for a description of each system.
**The least-cost county solid wastes disposal system.

Table F-7. Total Annual Cost for Alternative Solid Wastes System, City of Evansville, Indiana, 1971

Disposal System*	Total Annual Disposal System Cost (dollars)	Disposal System*	Total Annual Disposal System Cost (dollars)
1	1,964,849.96	10	2,205,293.65
2	1,954,344.81	11	2,034,277.31
3**	1,913,980.44	12	1,999,261.30
5	1,982,535.73	13	2,097,386.93
6	1,987,110.76	14	2,131,835.50
7	2,022,447.18	15	1,965,528.82
8	2,045,397.60	16	1,980,996.20
9	2,151,584.87		

*See Table 5-2 for a description of each system.
**The least-cost county solid wastes disposal system.

References

Alexander, R.M., G.D. Smith, and J.V. Walters, *Chilton County Solid Waste Disposal Demonstration Project Detailed Progress Report*, Project Clean and Green, Clanton, Alabama, 1971.

Alexander, R.M. and J.V. Walters, *Chilton County Landfill Summary Report for Initiation Year*, Project Clean and Green, Clanton, Alabama, 1969.

Alexander, R.M. and J.V. Walters, *Clean and Green* (monograph), The Board of Revenue and Control and the Municipalities of Chilton County, Alabama, Clanton, Alabama, 1969.

Bleuer, N.K., *Geologic Considerations in Planning Solid-Waste Disposal Sites in Indiana*, Environmental Study 1, Geological Survey Special Report 5, Department of Natural Resources, State of Indiana, Bloomington, Indiana, 1970.

Clayton, K.C., *A Methodlogy for Determining the Least-Cost Size, Number and Location of Solid Waste Disposal Sites*, Urban Economics Report No. 40, The University of Chicago, 1970.

Clayton, K.C., *An Evaluation of the Economic Feasibility of a Regional Solid Wastes System for the Southwestern Indiana and Kentucky Council of Governments Region*, Unpublished Masters Thesis, Department of Agricultural Economics, Purdue University, West Lafayette, Indiana, 1972.

Friedrich, C.J., *Alfred Weber's Theory of the Location of Industries*, University of Chicago Press, Chicago, 1928.

Golueke, C.G. and P.H. McGauhey, "First Annual Report," *Comprehensive Studies of Solid Waste Management—First and Second Annual Reports*, U.S. Department of Health, Education and Welfare, Public Health Service, Environmental Health Service, Bureau of Solid Waste Management, 1970.

Greenhut, M., *Plant Location in Theory and in Practice—The Economics of Space*, The University of North Carolina Press, Chapel Hill, North Carolina, 1956.

Haug, L., "When Does Transfer Pay Off?," *Refuse Removal Journal*, Vol. 19: No. 8, pp. 52-54.

Havlicek, J., R. Richardson, and L. Davies, *Measuring the Impacts of Solid Waste Disposal Site Location on Property Values*, Urban Economics Report No. 65, The University of Chicago, 1971.

Havlicek, J., G.S. Tolley, and Y. Wang, "Solid Wastes—A Resource?", *American Journal of Agricultural Economics*, Vol. 51: No. 5, pp. 1598-1602.

Henderson, J.M. and R.E. Quandt, *Microeconomic Theory—A Mathematical Approach*, McGraw-Hill Book Company, New York, 1958.

Henningson, Durham & Richardson, Inc., *Collection and Disposal of Solid Waste for the Des Moines Metropolitan Area*, U.S. Department of Health, Education and Welfare, Public Health Service, Environmental Control Administration, Solid Wastes Program, Cincinnati, 1968.

Hoover, E.M., *The Location of Economic Activity*, McGraw-Hill, New York, 1948.

Hotelling, H., "Stability in Competition," *The Economic Journal*, Vol. 39: No. 153, pp. 41-57.

Huie, J.M., *Solid Waste Management—Storage, Collection and Disposal*, Cooperative Extension Service, Purdue University, Lafayette, Indiana, 1970.

Isard, W., *Location and Space Economy*, John Wiley & Sons, Inc., 1956.

Johnston, J., *Statistical Cost Analysis,* McGraw-Hill Book Company, Inc., New York, 1960.

Lewis, J.P., *An Introduction to Mathematics*, St. Martin's Press, New York, 1965.

Lin, A. and E.O. Heady, "Empirical Cost Functions for Labour-Intensive Paddy Farms in Formosa", *The Australian Journal of Agricultural Economics*, Vol. 14: No. 2, pp. 138-149.

Losch, A., *The Economics of Location*, as translated by William H. Woglom and Wolfgang F. Stolper, Yale University Press, New Haven, Connecticut, 1964.

Morse, N. and E.W. Roth, *Systems Analysis of Regional Solid Waste Handling*, U.S. Department of Health, Education and Welfare, Public Health Service, Environmental Health Service, Bureau of Solid Waste Management, 1970.

Moses, L., "Location and the Theory of Production," *Quarterly Journal of Economics*, Vol. 73, pp. 259-272.

Muhich, A.J., A.J. Klee, and P.W. Britton, *Preliminary Data Analysis—1968 National Survey of Community Solid Waste Practices*, Public Health Service Publication No. 1867, Washington, U.S. Government Printing Office, 1968.

National Association of Counties Research Foundation, *Solid Waste Management—Design and Operation (No. 5)*, U.S. Department of Health, Education and Welfare, Public Health Service, Consumer Protection and Environmental Health Service, Environmental Control Administration, Bureau of Solid Waste Management, 1969.

Noonan, R. and A. Whinston, "An Information System for Vehicle Scheduling," *Software Age*, December 1969, pp. 8-13.

Preliminary Draft of a Soil Conservation Service Publication on Sanitary Landfills, 1971.

Reed, R., *Plant Location, Layout and Maintenance*, The Irwin Series in Operations Management, Richard D. Irwin, Inc., Homewood, Illinois, 1967.

Roe, T.L., *Optimal Spatial Distribution and Size of Cattle Slaughtering Plants in Indiana*, Unpublished Ph.D. Thesis, Purdue University, Lafayette, Indiana, 1969.

Samuelson, P.A., *Foundations of Economic Analysis*, Atheneum, New York, 1967.

Scherer, J., "Pollution and Environmental Control," *Federal Reserve Bank of New York—Monthly Review*, Vol. 53: No. 6, pp. 132-139.

Stollsteimer, J.F., "A Working Model for Plant Numbers and Locations," *Journal of Farm Economics*, Vol. 45: No. 3, pp. 631-645.

Teknatronic Applications, Inc., *Data Collection for Computer-Assisted School Bus Scheduling*, Lafayette, Indiana, 1970.

Toftner, R.O. and R.M. Clark, *Intergovernmental Approaches to Solid Waste Management*, U.S. Environmental Protection Agency, Solid Waste Management Office, 1971.

vonThunen, J.H., *Der Isolierte Staat in Beziechung auf Landwirtschaft und Nationalokonomic*, 3rd edition, Schumacker-Zardilin, Berlin, 1875.

Watson, D.S., *Price Theory and Its Uses*, Houghton Mifflin Company, New York, 1963.

Index

About the Authors

Kenneth C. Clayton received his B.S. degree from Rutgers University and his M.S. degree from Purdue University, both in agricultural economics. He is presently working toward the PhD degree in agricultural economics at Purdue University with an interest in resource economics and community development. His research has been primarily in the areas of solid waste management and community development. In addition to this book, the author has two other publications on the economics of solid waste management. He is a member of the American Agricultural Economics Association and the Community Development Society. He also holds membership in Alpha Zeta and Phi Kappa Phi.

John M. Huie is Associate Professor of Agricultural Economics and an Extension Economist at Purdue University. Dr. Huie, a graduate of Auburn and Michigan State Universities, has had over seven years of experience in Alabama and Indiana working with local leaders and governmental officials on a wide range of problems related to community services and facilities. Because of the importance of solid waste management during the recent years, considerable emphasis has been placed on this service. His responsibility with the Cooperative Extension Service in Alabama and Indiana has required that he apply his academic training to practical community problems at a level that is meaningful to the practitioner.

In addition to this book, he has two other publications related to solid waste, as well as publications in Local Government Finance, Industrial Location and Outdoor Recreation. Other areas of interest include financing public primary and secondary education, and state and local government tax structure.